Chicago Tribune

OUT OF THE
BLUE

THE REMARKABLE STORY OF
THE 2003 CHICAGO CUBS

Two lifelong baseball men, Don Zimmer (left) and Jerome Holtzman, talk in a Philadelphia dugout in 1989.

This book is dedicated to
Jerome Holtzman,
dean of American baseball writers,
who brought the joy of the game
to two generations of Chicago readers.

CONTENTS

DUSTY BAKER

'This is just the beginning'

Ialways felt it was preordained for me to come to Chicago. When my mother-in-law was on her deathbed a few years ago, she predicted I would wind up in Chicago. When the opportunity came up, I prayed on it, and I know it was the right decision. Who wouldn't want to be the manager or coach who was associated with a winner in Chicago?

I always enjoyed coming to Chicago when I played and managed elsewhere, but I was still surprised by the passion I found here. Chicago is just a great sports town. People eat, drink and sleep their Cubs, and their support was encouraging and gratifying. Wrigley Field was filled all year, and the number of fans who went on the road with us to Pittsburgh late in the season and to Atlanta and Florida for the playoffs . . . it was unbelievable to experience that.

I didn't expect to win a division title in the first year, to be honest. I was hoping for a winning season, and then another one because one of the things I kept hearing was the Cubs haven't had back-to-back winning seasons in so long. But our guys played hard all year, they overcame a lot, and they got themselves in position to win when the opportunity was there. I'm proud of them.

We're disappointed right now because we had an opportunity to go to the World Series, and it didn't happen for us. You're always disappointed when you come this close and don't get there, but that's how life is. We'll bounce back.

It was a good year. We accomplished a lot. People were really into it, but I think we gave them something to get into.

And in my mind, this is just the beginning. Good things are going to come for many years.

Dusty Baker

For once, the party went on all year
in the stands and on the rooftops
surrounding Wrigley Field

Paul Bako would miss this popup but not much else during the season.
By year's end, the fans were head over heels in love with the champion Cubs.

410

Corey Patterson's second year was cut short by injury, but
while he was on the field he made it all look easy.

Mark Grudzielanek and the Cubs left a lot of teams in their dust during 2003. Here he scores against the crosstown rival White Sox in June.

At the beginning of the year, some thought the season's highlight would be the Yankees series in early June. But the fun—and crowds—stuck around all summer.

MIKE DOWNEY

Unlikely season
worth the wait

At a so-called town hall meeting in Buffalo back in the spring of 2000, when Hillary Rodham Clinton was a candidate for the U.S. Senate, moderator Wolf Blitzer of CNN posed a difficult question with regard to whether she considered herself a true New Yorker.

"For example," she was asked, "suppose there was a World Series between the New York Yankees and the Chicago Cubs."

A true-blue Cubs fan since her upbringing in the Chicago suburbs, the former first lady handled this potential political hot potato with diplomacy and aplomb.

"Well, it's not a likely scenario," she said, drawing a laugh from the upstate New York audience, "but get back to me if it happens."

Ah, the life of a Cubs fan.

No pain, no gain.

It takes a village the size of Chicago to comprehend and overcome the many hardships of having a beloved team best known for its failings. A lovable loser, as it were. Baseball's version of Charlie Brown.

Having civic pride in the Yankees is easy. To be a New Yorker and declare that your baseball team is the best there is now and ever was—well, who in his or her right mind would dare to engage in a public debate? Particularly anyone with Chicago ties or roots?

"Chicago Cubs fans are the greatest fans in baseball," the team's long-ago manager, Herman Franks, once observed. "They've got to be."

Like a prizefighter who keeps getting up after getting knocked down, a Cubs fan does not throw in the towel. He or she keeps coming back for more. For more punishment. For more embarrassment. But for one more chance at that million-to-1 shot—swinging and finally connecting.

Because which man, woman or child truly devoted to the Cubs would care to be the one who abandoned them in their time of need? (Their time of need being 1908 to the present.)

You don't kick an underdog. You care for it, be kind to it. Particularly one as sad and hungry as the Cubs, who, if you think about it, are not so much America's team (as some have claimed to be) as they are America's underdog.

A theory has long existed, in fact, that if the Cubs, deprived for 95 years, did at last succeed, it would be the greatest day of many a life—the glory, glory hallelujah day—but simultaneously the undoing of this wildly popular organization's entire identity.

As in:

The losers finally won. Now what?

It was broached in 1984, when by defeating the San Diego Padres one more time the Cubs would have proceeded to the World Series with a shot at changing their sad-sack image forever.

Prolonging the agony instead by falling to the Padres 7-1, 7-5 and 6-3—not a one-run loss in the bunch—the sole residual benefit became that the "poor Cubs" remained just that, a team to feel sympathy for, a team to chuckle at, a team to stand by through thick and thin (mainly thin).

Grandparents still got to tell grandchildren, "Maybe next year."

Comedians still got to tell jokes.

Like a prizefighter who keeps
getting up after getting knocked down,
a Cubs fan does not throw in the towel. He or she
keeps coming back for more.

"There's less suicide among Cubs fans because we have something to live for," standup comic Tom Dreesen says of his favorite team. "I fear the day when the Cubs win the World Series. The following morning, 20,000 people will jump off Tribune Tower, because what's the use?"

One must choose one's poison. George Will, a conservative newspaper columnist and rabid base-ball fan, says that as a child he felt it necessary to decide between the Cubs and the St. Louis Cardinals as his favorite team. He chose the Cubs and has been among their steadfast but suffering minions ever since.

"All my Cardinal-fan friends grew up to be happy," Will once wrote. "And liberal."

But even a loyal left-winger can find room in the Cubs' rotation, as Hillary Clinton did when she threw out the ceremonial first pitch of the 1994 season at Wrigley Field.

As she told Newsweek in an interview that spring, "Being a Cubs fan prepares you for life—and Washington."

To her regret, there would be no White House ceremony in Washington during her husband's administration to honor a Cubs championship team. No photo op for Bill Clinton to be presented an appropriately monogrammed "C" cap and a Cubs jersey with No. 1 on the back.

But who knows? Perhaps someday in our lives President Clinton will be Hillary Clinton, and she will be the one in the Rose Garden celebrating the championship of the Cubs.

Not a likely scenario, but get back to her if it happens. ●

Will the Cubs win the World Series in Mike Downey's lifetime? Get back to him if it happens.

RICK MORRISSEY

A team with a little something extra

For most of the 2003 season, Dusty Baker tried to quarantine his players from all the wretched history, attempted to sequester them from Cubs fans' long memories, strove to shield them from the notion that they were part of an organization that was more voodoo pin cushion than baseball team.

How was he to know it was impossible? He was new to this.

One morning in early September, the Cubs' manager walked around the infield and outfield at Wrigley Field, sprinkling a gray, powdery substance. That was the day he finally got it. That was the day he finally understood that all that wretched history and all those long memories were bigger than he was, bigger than any motivational speech, bigger than any decision to turn to the bullpen.

Now no one wants to say this secret Dusty dust was the thing that nudged the Cubs into the playoffs. You'd like to think that when they finished ahead of the Astros in the National League Central Division, it was because of baseball ability and baseball smarts. No one wants to be that superstitious. We're too urbane for magic, too sophisticated.

But Cubs fans understand having all their bases covered, and if it was going to take some magic dust to take a whack at 95 years of misery, well, sprinkle away, Dusty. Besides, no one can say for sure that the unknown substance didn't suck up all the bad vibes and render them ineffective.

The important thing was that Baker was now officially one of them, having come to grips with the idea that if the season was going to play out the way he wanted it to, he was going to need

something a little bigger than four power pitchers and one power hitter. He was going to need a powder.

This was going to take something a little extra.

That was the theme of this season, wasn't it? A little something extra?

No, no. We're not talking about cork in the bat. Not that sort of extra. But come to think of it, that was part of it too. The Cubs needed a little something extra to overcome the loss of Sammy Sosa, who served a seven-game suspension in June for using a corked bat. They carried on without their star.

By no stretch of the imagination was this a wildly talented team. There was very good pitching, yes. There was Mark Prior, the 23-year-old who pitched like a 30-year-old Tom Seaver. There was Kerry Wood, who reaches out and touches greatness often enough that you don't dare look away when he pitches. Carlos Zambrano helped carry the team in August, and Matt Clement, still looking for more consistency, was more good than bad. The Cubs had an offensive force in Sosa.

But the club won a weak NL Central by one game over the Astros. The Cubs finished 88-74, not great by any measuring stick but a huge improvement over 2002, when they won just 67 games.

When it counted, they seemed to find a way. This team had a resiliency that had been missing in past Cubs teams. One bad game in previous seasons, one bad stretch and you could pretty much count on a prayer service and a burial. Not this season.

The recipe for this team was one part talent and two parts grit, with a pinch of that magic dust

"They've got some good guys here, some real good guys here, guys who come to play. Sure, we make mistakes. We don't look good sometimes, but this team can fight..."

thrown in. It stirred the city.

"[Resiliency is] part of it," Baker said toward the end of the season. "And I think the fact that the players stick together is part of it. They really have gotten close as a team. They pull for each other. I haven't seen any envy or jealousy that a lot of times heats up some clubs. It's like the plague; you can't stop it sometimes.

"They've got some good guys here, some real good guys here, guys who come to play. Sure, we make mistakes. We don't look good sometimes, but this team can fight, no matter what the score is, no matter what the situation is."

Most observers didn't expect the Cubs to finish where they did, atop the Central, so there was a tendency to underestimate their chances in the postseason or to believe they had accomplished enough. Baker would have none of it.

That was a huge part of the equation with the Cubs. Baker refused to talk about what couldn't be done here or why things hadn't worked here in the past. A lot of managers had blown through town spouting a similar can-do message, but few were able to open minds and ear canals the way Baker did.

"Why not us?" Baker said when he was hired in November.

A very good question that turned out to be an answer: Why not the Cubs, indeed?

And Baker's secret substance? He refused to reveal what it was until after the season ended. But on that day in September, after Baker had sprinkled his magic dust on Wrigley Field, the Cubs came back from a six-run deficit to beat the St. Louis Cardinals 8-7.

You decide what that means. Just don't argue about the results. ●

Magic dust was only a small part of what Rick Morrissey witnessed with the Cubs this season.

FIRST INNING

DUSTY'S ROAD

AS THE CLOCK ran out on Bruce Kimm's interim tenure as Cubs manager late in the 2002 season, rumors surfaced that the Cubs wanted Dusty Baker to replace him. ❦ Skeptics—and they are legion among "long-suffering" Cubs fans—scoffed. A ploy to divert attention from a miserable 95-loss season, they

grumbled. Baker was big-time, a star, too high-profile for the Cubs, who seemed to prefer putting unobtrusive baseball lifer types named Jim in charge of the dugout ... Jim Frey, Jim Essian, Jim Riggleman.

Rock-solid Don Baylor was a notable exception. He had achieved stature as a player and had been reasonably successful as the Colorado Rockies' manager. But his two-year Cubs tenure had ended badly, the old "failure to communicate" bugaboo blamed for chronic underachievement. After Kimm failed to improve the situation, Jim Hendry set his sights high. He knew his first major decision as Cubs general manager would be his most important in terms of setting the tone for what he hoped to achieve--an unequivocal end to decades of frustration.

Baker was wrapping up a heady 10-year run in San Francisco with the Giants' first World Series appearance since 1989. He'd taken the team to the postseason two other times, won three Manager of the Year Awards and achieved detente with prickly personalities such as Barry Bonds and Jeff

Kent. He also had become a Bay Area icon.

But as the owners who had hired him came to resent his popularity, Baker began to feel unappreciated. He was ready for a fresh challenge, and in baseball, none was bigger than reversing the fortunes of a franchise that seemed downtrodden by its very birthright. On Nov. 19, 2002, Hendry introduced Baker as the Cubs' 55th manager.

"It's pretty obvious that he's one of the best in the business," Hendry said. "He gets the most out of every player who plays for him."

Hendry, impatient by nature, was eager to start his rebuilding project. But he didn't mind waiting a few weeks, convinced as he was that he had the right man.

"All along, Jim's first choice was Dusty Baker," said Cubs President Andy MacPhail, who signed off on the atypically hefty expenditure. "His second choice was Dusty Baker, and his third choice was Dusty Baker. He clearly felt Dusty was what this organization needed, and he stayed with it."

Baker was characteristically charm-

ing and affable as he met the media at Wrigley Field and humble in insisting he was "no miracle worker." Above all, he was adamant that the status quo was about to change. There are no "lovable losers" in his world. "I'm here to win," he said, and he repeated it often enough to leave no doubt as to his intentions.

"I've been handed a few seemingly impossible tasks in my life," Baker said. "But this is a situation any manager or coach would dream of–winning in Chicago."

He didn't want to hear about billy goats, curses, day games or any of the other excuses that had been put forth annually as impediments to the Cubs. "All that happened before I got here," Baker said.

He didn't want to hear about Cubs fans being more interested in Wrigley Field's social ambience than in the quality of the baseball played there. He'd been there often enough as an opposing player and manager to recognize passion, and he knew what was needed to ignite it.

"I'm here to win," Baker said. There was no doubt he meant it. ●

When Dusty Baker
came on board,
Cubs fans strapped
themselves in for a
wild, exciting ride.

When Baker decided to make his views known, there was never any doubt about what he was trying to say.

Baker and Shawn Estes were reunited in Chicago after spending years together in San Francisco. At the end of the season, Estes would come through with his best game for his skipper.

Baker quickly became a fan favorite. Darren Baker, age 4, was a fan favorite too.

Darren Baker wasn't the Cubs' batboy in 2003, but he was never too far away from the action.

Talk to his players and one thing comes clear: Baker is a master at knowing when to give them a kick–start, and when to play it cool. Here he thanks Kerry Wood for his draining effort against the White Sox.

From day one of spring training, Dusty Baker's message was clear. The losing was over—he had come to Chicago to win.

A NEW LOOK

NOT THAT IT curbed their enthusiasm toward him, but Cubs officials accepted Dusty Baker's declaration that he wasn't a miracle man when they hired him in November 2002. So they set out to improve a roster that lost 95 games the previous season. ❧ General manager Jim Hendry's best

move was so one-sided that it resembled Brock-for-Broglio … only it favored the Cubs. Hendry got the Dodgers to take catcher Todd Hundley, whose dream of signing with his hometown team had turned into a nightmare, in exchange for veterans Eric Karros and Mark Grudzielanek.

Hundley, son of former Cubs stalwart Randy Hundley, signed a four-year, $24 million free-agent contract before the 2001 season but left his hitting stroke somewhere between Los Angeles and Chicago. He didn't help himself by responding negatively to the taunts of Wrigley Field fans who turned on him as his productivity failed to justify his paycheck.

The Cubs did him a favor by moving him. Getting useful players in return was an unexpected bonus.

Karros was a consistent, productive hitter through the late 1990s, but the Dodgers grew concerned that back problems had robbed him of his power. Grudzielanek, the embodiment of country hardball, had paid a physical price for years of aggressive, all-out play, but the Cubs liked him as insurance in case second baseman Bobby

Hill wasn't ready for full-time duty.

Hill wasn't, and Grudzielanek stepped in to become one of the Cubs' most valuable players. Karros, meanwhile, was a calm, veteran presence who provided some big hits in his role as a platoon first baseman with Hee Seop Choi and Randall Simon.

Hundley's departure also created an opening behind the plate … two openings after the Cubs decided they had to do better than light-hitting Joe Girardi. So they upgraded substantially by dealing two prospects to Arizona for Damian Miller and one to Milwaukee for Paul Bako.

The Cubs' bullpen was worse than bad in 2002. It was embarrassing, blowing more saves (25) than it converted (23). Things looked bleak when Antonio Alfonseca, the team's only established closer, tore a hamstring in spring training. Journeyman Joe Borowski, owner of two career saves, got first crack at the job and never relinquished it, getting hitters out without doing anything flashy.

Baker's reputation as a players' manager paid dividends when Mike Remlinger signed as a free agent.. The

hard-throwing left-hander had established himself in Atlanta as one of the National League's best setup men, and he carried himself with the confidence that winning instills. Baker used him in the stickiest situations, often as a complement to soft-tossing fellow lefty Mark Guthrie. Kyle Farnsworth and veteran Dave Veres offered a similar fire-and-ice alternative from the right side.

Center–fielder Corey Patterson had chafed under Don Baylor's tough-love approach, but Baker's unwavering and oft-stated belief in him unlocked Patterson's vast potential.

Thus the Cubs broke camp in Mesa with Miller and Bako behind the plate, a Karros-Choi platoon at first base, Grudzielanek at second, Alex Gonzalez at shortstop, Mark Bellhorn at third and Patterson in center field, flanked by Moises Alou and Sammy Sosa. Tom Goodwin, Troy O'Leary and versatile Ramon Martinez were the extra men.

It wasn't the '75 Reds, and the roster would change during the season, but it was an improvement over 2002.

"I like our club," Baker said. "I think we're going to surprise some people." ●

One of the questions going into the season was whether Mark Prior would be as good as advertised. By the end of the season, that had been answered, and then some.

Pitcher Joe Borowski had been best known for a poor spot start against the Giants in 2001. But by the end of the year, he would be the Cubs' undisputed closer.

New faces, from left: Catcher Paul Bako, pitchers Mike Remlinger, Mark Guthrie and Dave Veres.

Damian Miller, who had caught Curt Schilling and Randy Johnson while he was with the Arizona Diamondbacks, got a chance to catch a new generation of aces with the Cubs.

Mike Remlinger, a veteran of playoff runs with the Atlanta Braves, was one of the first to sign on with the Cubs. The lefthander would help solidify the bullpen.

Eric Karros wore Dodger blue for most of his major league career, but his new uniform looked like a perfect fit to Cubs fans.

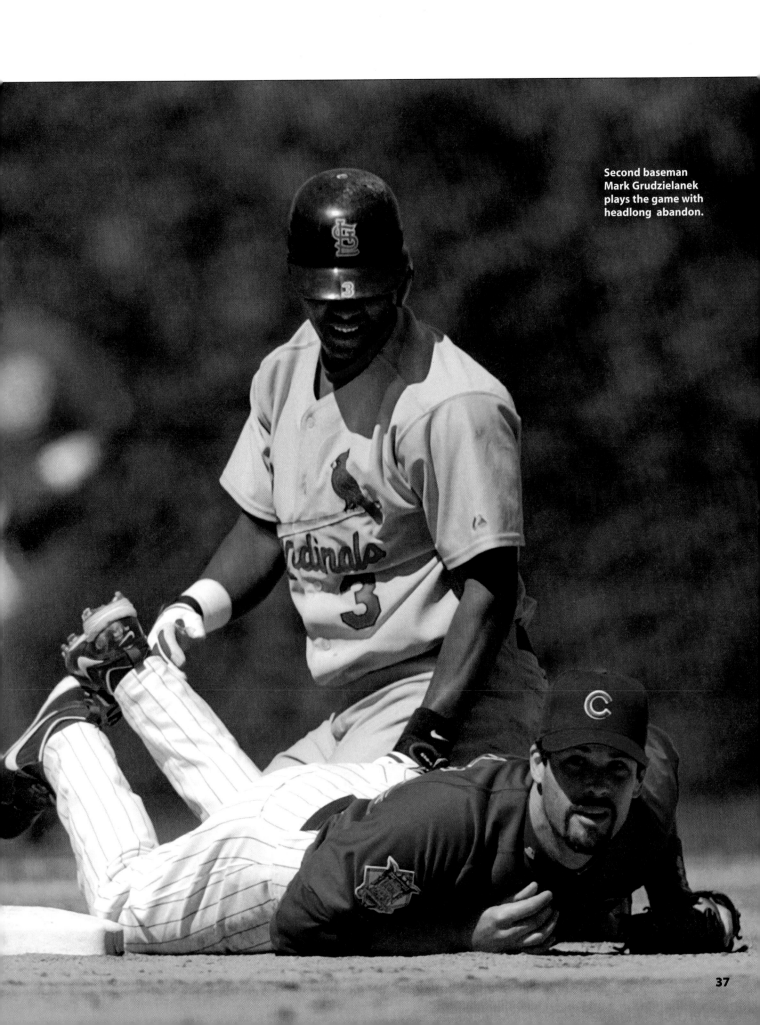

Second baseman
Mark Grudzielanek
plays the game with
headlong abandon.

37

Father and son: Sammy Sosa and Sammy Jr. share a moment during batting practice at Wrigley Field.

THIRD INNING

STILL THE MAN

THE PITCH—a high and tight fastball from Pittsburgh's Salomon Torres on April 20—set off a chain of events that no one could have predicted for Sammy Sosa, the Cubs' superstar right–fielder. ❧ Torres' pitch shattered Sosa's helmet and left him with three small cuts where fragments of plastic had smashed into

his face. He didn't miss a game and was back in the lineup two nights later, but he slumped through much of April. Then came toenail surgery, a trip to the disabled list, a last-minute online voting surge that left him off the All-Star team, an ejection for "cursing myself" and another beaning. His statistics dipped after five years of superhuman production.

And with one swing on a warm June night, Sosa shattered his bat and part of his sparkling image. He had used an illegal corked bat in a game, and though he swore it was an honest mistake, Sosa was suspended for seven games. The picture of an umpire inspecting Sosa's tainted lumber would be one of the season's enduring images.

Despite the injuries, the controversies and the first sustained criticism in his career, Sosa said he had the time of his life in 2003. Hitting his 500th home run on April 4 was only part of the excitement.

"It's unbelievable," he said. "A great team. It's awesome. That's how you win divisions and championships. Don't focus on one guy. Everybody has to do

it together."

Thanks to a reconstructed lineup and a four-star rotation, Sosa learned he could be a big part of the party without being the party by himself. "We have so many good players here I don't have to go up there trying to kill myself," he said in late September. "I know I have a lot of help, something I didn't have before, so I'm very happy about it."

Sosa was hardened somewhat by the reaction to his corked-bat incident, embittered by what he thought was media overkill. He said reporters treated his infraction as if he had committed a felony. All told, Sosa missed 20 games because of the toe injury and his suspension.

"It has been a difficult year for him," manager Dusty Baker said. "But then I look up and see he has 35 home runs, and if he hadn't missed those 20 games, there's a good chance he'd be the home run king again. ... He still has had a very good year."

Doug Glanville, who joined the Cubs in midseason, remembered the Sosa who played alongside him during his previous tenure with the Cubs, in 1997.

In those days, Sosa was considered a very good player with a penchant for hitting home runs and striking out.

Now Sosa is a certain Hall of Famer who by season's end had hit 40 home runs and moved into 10th place on the all-time list with 539. "It's different," Glanville said. "He still is a tremendous entertainer. ... He uses the whole field, he's hitting off-speed [pitches]. ... He was just hitting his stride when I left."

As it was for most of the previous decade, Sosa remained the focal point on the Cubs, despite the emergence of Mark Prior as a dominant starting pitcher and the continued excellence of Kerry Wood.

Sosa remained one of the guys in the clubhouse, where his boom box blasts Eminem and Whitney Houston whether he's in the room or not, sometimes leading to good-natured jabs from veteran teammates with more eclectic tastes. "How about a little Anita Baker?" Eric Karros asked one day.

Could Dusty Baker picture the day when Sosa no longer would be the Cubs' right–fielder? The answer was simple: "No." ●

Sosa swore he had used the illegal bat by mistake, and that he had it only because he wanted to use it to put on a show for the fans in batting practice.

Some fans quickly forgave Sosa, but for most of the year opponents' fans – like this White Sox supporter – wouldn't let him forget the corked-bat incident.

The swing that shocked the world: Sosa used an illegally corked bat against Tampa Bay in June. When it shattered, he was ejected from the game and later would be suspended for seven games.

Sosa likes to refer to himself as a gladiator. Here he gets ready to enter the arena before a spring training game.

Sosa says he does whatever it takes to help the Cubs win, even if it means putting in a little vine time.

After all the controversy and injury, Sosa got back to doing what he does best: Slugging home runs. He would wind up the season in 10th place on the all-time home run list with 539.

YANKEES, GO HOME

WRIGLEY FIELD WAS the center of the baseball universe from June 6-8. Longtime patrons of the old North Side ballyard couldn't remember it being more revved up than it was for the New York Yankees' first visit since the 1938 World Series. ❦ Even the players were caught up in the excitement. "I've

never been on this field before," said Derek Jeter, the Yankees' captain and shortstop. "I grew up in Michigan and I'm a history buff, so this is exciting for me."

Jason Giambi, who had awed the crowd by hitting one bomb after another onto Sheffield Avenue during batting practice, kept slugging when Game 1 started. His two-run homer helped the Yankees and David Wells to a 5-3 victory. "This is exciting," Giambi said. "The fans are really into it, and the buzz in the air was definitely a playoff-type atmosphere."

By Saturday the buzz was as loud as a jet engine. Kerry Wood would pitch Game 2 for the Cubs, facing fellow Texan Roger Clemens, his boyhood idol who was seeking his 300th career victory. The much-anticipated showdown lived up to its billing, interspersed with an anxious moment.

Wood seemed to have his best stuff but trailed 1-0 after giving up a home run to Hideki Matsui on a hanging slider in the fifth inning. In the fourth, the Cubs were employing a drastic shift against

Giambi when the Yankees' cleanup hitter lofted a popup in front of the plate. Catcher Damian Miller never saw it and third baseman Lenny Harris couldn't get to it, so Wood and first baseman Hee Seop Choi gave chase.

Wood, thinking he'd overrun the ball, came to an abrupt stop. Choi ran into him, falling to the ground and landing on his head with a sickening thud, unconscious. An eerie silence settled over the crowd as an ambulance rolled onto the field through a gate in the right-field wall. Wood, unhurt but shaken, looked on from one knee near third base.

After 17 minutes that seemed more like an hour, Choi's eyes fluttered open. As the rookie was loaded into the ambulance, manager Dusty Baker handed him the ball he'd held on to that had retired Giambi.

There was still a game to win. Baker visited the mound and told Wood to "cowboy up" and win it for Choi.

And Wood did, with some help from Eric Karros and Mike Remlinger.

Clemens, weakened by a bronchial infection, left with a 1-0 lead after the

Cubs' first two hitters reached base in the seventh inning. Juan Acevedo relieved him, and Karros, who had taken over for Choi, hit the first pitch into the left-field seats to give the Cubs the lead.

Wood struck out 11 and gave up only three hits but left after loading the bases in the eighth. On came Remlinger to strike out Giambi and preserve the Cubs' victory. "I've been in big games, playoff games, and this game had as much emotion as any game I've ever played in," Karros said.

In Sunday's finale, Moises Alou hit a three-run homer in the first inning and the Cubs chased eventual 21-game winner Andy Pettitte in the second. They hung on to win 8-7 when closer Joe Borowski picked pinch-runner Charles Gipson off first base for the final out.

The Cubs took two of three, ending a 6-6 homestand that featured Sammy Sosa's corked-bat controversy. "You don't know if this is a defining moment or a turning point until down the road," Baker said. "It's hard to see it as a turning point when you're in the middle of chaos." ●

Roger Clemens was trying to win his 300th game against the Cubs in Wrigley Field. Thanks to Kerry Wood and Eric Karros, he wouldn't.

The Bombers are back: The New York series was the first matchup between the Cubs and the Yankees since the 1938 World Series.

Mike Remlinger struck out Jason Giambi with the bases loaded to end the eighth inning of Game 2, bringing the crowd to its feet.

The collision: Kerry Wood and Hee Seop Choi crash into each other going for a pop fly against the Yankees.

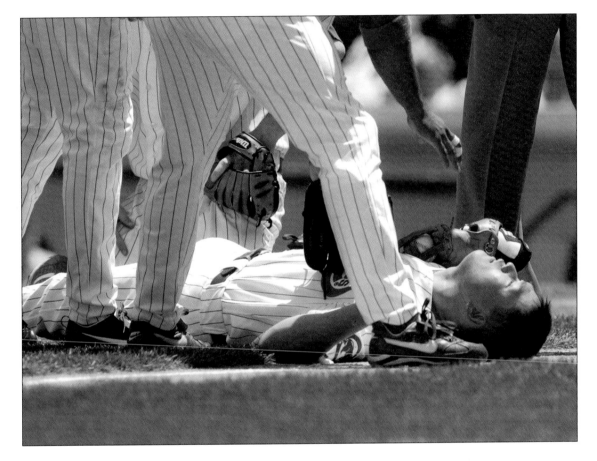

After colliding with Wood, Choi lay on the ground for several minutes before his eyes blinked open. As he left the field, Baker would hand him the baseball he had caught.

Charles Gipson couldn't bear to watch after Joe Borowski picked him off first to end the final game of the series.

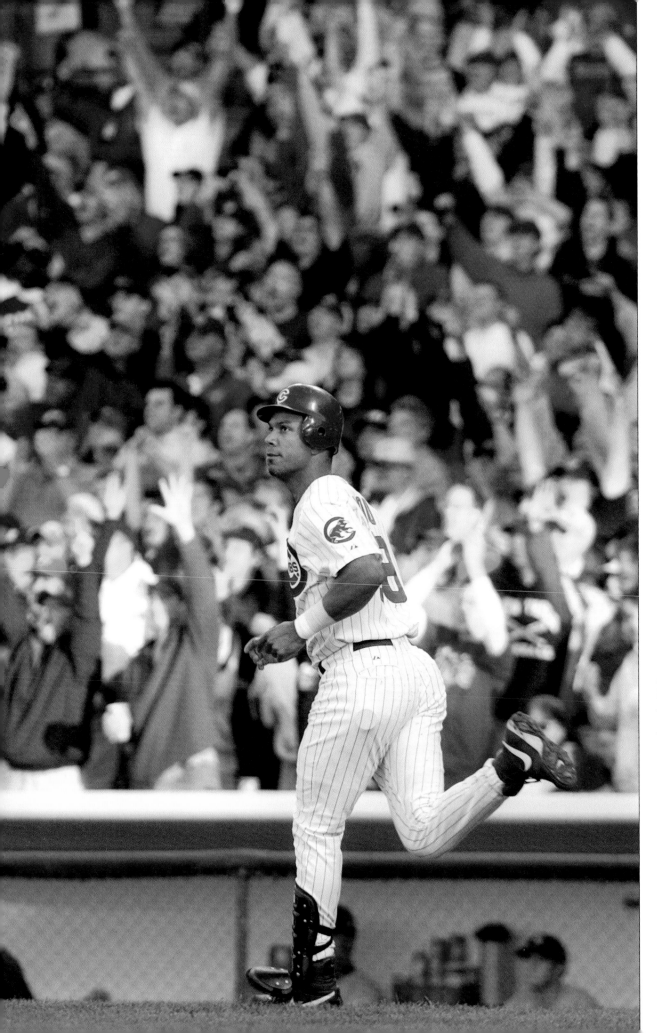

In a series of big hits, Moises Alou's three-run home run was one of the biggest.

Kenny Lofton came over from Pittsburgh after Corey Patterson's injury and instantly gave the Cubs the leadoff hitter they needed.

REINFORCEMENTS

THE CUBS STARTED the season with what appeared to be a youth movement well under way. Their center–fielder was second-year player Corey Patterson, a speedster with remarkable power for a small man. First base was earmarked for rookie Hee Seop Choi, a large left-handed power hitter from

Korea. Third base, a continual problem for the Cubs since the departure of Ron Santo, was handed to Mark Bellhorn, a switch-hitter who had smacked a surprising 27 home runs in 2002.

By mid-August, all three would be gone. Bellhorn never found his stroke again and was traded to Colorado in June. Choi seemingly never recovered from a collision with pitcher Kerry Wood during the Yankees series the first weekend of June and was sent back to the minors in August. And Patterson, easily the Cubs' best player in the first half of the season, blew out his knee in early July and was done for the season.

Along came the cavalry the players who ride into town as the result of mid-season trades, hoping they are the right reinforcements to guarantee a championship season.

Three came from the Pittsburgh Pirates, a franchise that was clearing the decks to save salaries. Kenny Lofton took over for Patterson in center, adding speed and a veteran presence in the clubhouse. It didn't hurt that he grew up as a Cubs fan in East Chicago, Ind., and was a Dusty Baker

fan as well, having played for him as the Giants made their World Series run in 2002.

"My family was pretty excited about me playing for the Cubs," Lofton said.

The Lofton trade also brought Aramis Ramirez, a 25-year-old third baseman who had shown flashes of brilliance with the Pirates in 2001. But he had slumped in 2002, and when he arrived in town he already had committed 23 errors. He booted another in his first game in Chicago.

But Ramirez would provide clutch hitting and another home-run threat in the lineup. He would finish with 27 home runs and 106 RBIs.

Then came Randall Simon, a first baseman who had achieved some notoriety earlier in the season when he jokingly struck a participant in Milwaukee's famous "sausage race" with a bat. He paid a $432 fine, but he really made his amends on the field after arriving in mid-August, providing left-handed power off the bench and platooning at first base with Eric Karros, a right-handed hitter.

Other late additions were outfielder Doug Glanville, a former Cub acquired

from Texas in late July, and Tony Womack, who came from Colorado and provided insurance after second baseman Mark Grudzielanek broke his right hand in August. Both brought speed and outstanding defensive skills to the lineup, giving Baker the ability to protect a late-inning lead or give a needed day off to a starter down the stretch.

The architect of it all was Jim Hendry, the general manager in his first full season on the job. In all, Hendry added six position players to the team's roster after June 19 (Jose Hernandez, acquired that day, wound up as trade bait). For all the new Cubs, being traded from teams that were mired deep in their division to the contending Cubs was nothing less than a midsummer's dream.

"Going someplace where you're wanted, that's all that matters to me, knowing that what you bring to the table helps them," said Womack, who hit a game-winning single in the tumultuous Cardinals series in early September. "When you're on the bench somewhere and you're traded and you're wanted, that's pretty much the best feeling ever."

Walking on air: Corey Patterson scored on Alex Gonzalez's single in the ninth inning to beat the Cardinals in July. But when Patterson went out for the season with a knee injury, the Cubs had to go shopping.

Aramis Ramirez was known as a powerful but erratic hitter and a so-so fielder when he arrived from Pittsburgh. But he found consistency at the plate in Chicago and was better with the glove than anyone expected.

Randall Simon and Kenny Lofton were mired with a losing team in Pittsburgh. When they came to the Cubs, the teammates were with a winner and dancing for joy.

Off with the pitch, Kenny Lofton hesitates between second and third base to make sure that Moises Alou's home run blast will clear the wall. Lofton and Alex Gonzalez often were the 1-2 punch at the top of the lineup, charged with getting on base so they could be driven in by sluggers Sammy Sosa and Alou.

ACE OF CUBS

YOU COULD HAVE forgiven Cubs fans if they saw a championship season flashing before their eyes on the afternoon of July 11. In fact, you could have forgiven them if they thought the next decade would be ruined as well. ❦ Mark Prior, the Cubs' best young pitcher since Kerry Wood, had run into Atlanta

second baseman Marcus Giles on the basepaths, somersaulting over Giles and crashing onto his pitching shoulder. He winced and gripped his arm as the Wrigley Field crowd held its breath. Giles was knocked cold. Both players had to be helped from the field.

Giles suffered a concussion and missed the All-Star Game the next week at U.S. Cellular Field. Prior made the game but didn't pitch. Though Prior said he was only bruised and could pitch, his soreness lingered. On July 21, he was placed on the 15-day disabled list. Again, Chicago fans held their breath.

But when he came back ... whew.

After missing three starts, Prior reeled off seven victories in a row, giving up only six runs in the process. He lost a tight game to the Montreal Expos in San Juan, Puerto Rico, then won three more down the stretch, including a 4-2 victory over the Pirates on the day the Cubs clinched the division. Prior wasn't just the best young pitcher in the major leagues anymore. For the second half of the season, he

was the best pitcher, period.

"It's a joke is what it is, for someone that young to be that polished and to have that kind of composure and just really be that dominant," said first baseman Eric Karros in the middle of that run.

This was the sort of performance Cubs fans expected when Prior was taken with the second overall pick in the 2001 draft. But even the most optimistic fan didn't expect him to be so good so soon. The big right-hander with oversized calves had all the tools a rocketing fastball, a sharp-breaking curve and the ability to place either pitch precisely where he wanted it. But no one could have predicted his maturity. General manager Jim Hendry said Prior was "more mature at his age than any player I've ever seen," and his teammates backed that up by electing him player representative.

Because he came out of the University of Southern California and because of his live fastball, he often was compared with another Trojan, Tom Seaver. Because of his tenacity, others thought of him as an heir to

Curt Schilling. His control brought to mind Mike Mussina. And his curve? Think Dwight Gooden.

Any doubts about his toughness on the mound were erased early. On May 1, Giants slugger Barry Bonds, fresh off a two-homer performance the day before, strode to the plate with his team leading 1-0. Prior plunked him in the hand.

Bonds roared and snorted and began stalking toward the mound, a sight to quail almost any pitcher. Prior would have none of it. He took a step toward Bonds himself, throwing up his hand and tossing out a few words of his own as both benches cleared.

"I'm not backing down to him at all," Prior said later. "He's a good player, but just because he's been around 15 or 20 years and has 600 home runs doesn't mean I've got to stop doing what makes me successful."

All this came from a young man who had pitched only one year of professional baseball going into his magical season. He would not turn 23 until Sept. 7, and by that time, he was on top of the world. ●

Cubs fans always suspected Mark Prior would be special, but in 2003 he really gave them something to shout about.

Fans in the bleachers give their hero's name a unique and appropriate spelling.

The windup and delivery looked so effortless, but hitting Mark Prior's best stuff was anything but easy to the rest of the National League.

A sight that Cubs fans are expecting to see many times in the years to come: Kerry Wood and Mark Prior at the All-Star Game, chatting with pitching coach Larry Rothschild.

After a solid start and a frightenin
collision on the base paths, Mark Prie
started winning and never looked bac

DECKING THE CARDS

ON LABOR DAY, Sept. 1, fans saw a familiar scenario on their sports pages. The St. Louis Cardinals led the Cubs in the National League Central. ❦ But the Cubs were just 2 games behind the first-place Cards, and St. Louis was heading into Chicago for a five-game series that likely would determine whether

these Cubs would stick around for the rest of the season. Chicago was coming off a heartbreaking 2-0 loss to the usually woeful Milwaukee Brewers, while the Cardinals were riding the bat of MVP candidate Albert Pujols.

A week before, the Cubs had lost a painful two of three to the Cardinals in St. Louis, blowing one lead for Kerry Wood and losing the final game on a walkoff home run by Kerry Robinson. As the Cubs trudged off the field, they saw their archrivals bouncing in celebration at home plate.

Dark clouds and heavy rain postponed the opening game of the rematch for 4 hours 17 minutes, as 38,410 fans waited. When the rain passed, Mark Prior parted the clouds.

Pitching on an extra day of rest, Prior shut down the Cardinals for the second time in a week, allowing just five hits in eight innings to earn his sixth straight victory. The Cubs' numb bats woke up in the fifth inning, scoring six runs. Prior drove in a run himself in a 7-0 victory.

The next day was historic for Chicago baseball. The Cubs played a day-night doubleheader and the White Sox played Boston at home. In all, a record 95,223 fans watched games in the Windy City that day.

The day game was the sort of contest that made Cubs fans think it might just be their year. Tied 2-2 going into the bottom of the ninth, the Cubs got two singles, two walks and a stolen base and still failed to score, thanks to a baserunning blunder by Moises Alou and a tremendous catch by Cardinals left fielder Orlando Palmeiro.

Other Cubs teams might have faded. But the bullpen hung on, and Sammy Sosa smacked a two-run walkoff home run in the 15th inning to win it 4-2. "I got one pitch to hit, and that was everything," Sosa explained.

Sosa took a seat for the nightcap, but the Cubs could have used him. Wood allowed only one earned run but angered the Cardinals by nearly hitting pitcher Matt Morris twice. Managers Dusty Baker and Tony La Russa would jaw at each other for the rest of the series. But the worst confrontation came between the Cubs and the umpires.

Trailing 2-0 in the seventh, the Cubs loaded the bases with two outs. Alou appeared to make amends for his mistake in the day game by scorching a line drive down the third-base line that kicked up chalk, apparently tying the game. But umpire Justin Klemm called it foul, and Alou popped out to end the inning.

Relief pitcher Antonio Alfonseca charged Klemm between innings, bumping the umpire, and Alou added a rant of his own. Both were ejected, and Alfonseca would be suspended for seven games. But the worst news of all was the Cubs would lose 2-0.

Alou was back the next day with a vengeance, going 5-for-5 and driving in four runs in a come-from-behind 8-7 victory. "This is what we have to do for us to be a championship team," he said.

A little bit of magic may have helped. Early that morning, Baker had walked around the infield and outfield, scattering small handfuls of a dirtlike substance. He vowed not to reveal what was in the bag until after it had served its purpose, perhaps giving the Cubs a little something extra.

And in the series finale, the magic was there again. The teams traded the lead three times before Tony Womack drove in Alou with the winning run in a 7-6 victory. "If you're not a fan and you watched this series, you became a fan," Womack said.

The Cubs had won four of five, letting their fans believe that, indeed, this team might be something special. And the Cardinals never would threaten again. ●

When the Cubs finished taking four of five from the Cardinals in September, Sammy Sosa and Kenny Lofton couldn't help but jump for joy.

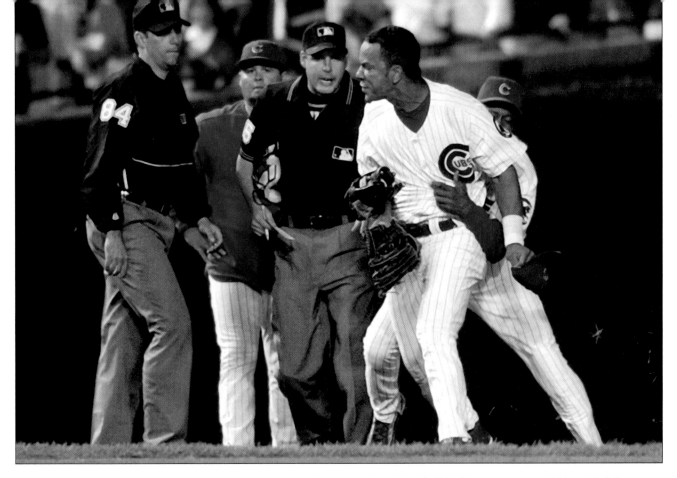

Moises Alou had to be restrained after the umpire called his late-inning line drive foul during Game 2. It would have tied the game.

Carlos Zambrano couldn't bear to watch after giving up a home run to Jim Edmonds in Game 1 of the Cardinals series. But the Cubs would win 4-2 in 15 innings.

Matt Morris ducks out of the way of a Kerry Wood pitch in Game 2. The bad blood would simmer for the rest of the series.

There was no doubt about the tension in the series – Dusty Baker escorted Randall Simon away from the plate after an argument with the umpire.

Alou would come back to star in the rest of the series, delivering clutch hitting and even going 5 for 5 in one game.

Kerry Wood mows
down the Mets during
a mid-September
four-hit shutout.

EIGHTH INNING

KID K GROWS UP

KERRY WOOD FIRED strike three past Jeff Kent to end the top of the seventh inning of the Cubs-Houston game on Aug. 11 at Wrigley Field, then strode off the mound to a roaring ovation. The strikeout was the 1,000th of his career, a milestone he had reached sooner than any other big-league pitcher.

Wood long has been a Wrigley Field favorite, and the capacity crowd kept chanting his name after he reached the dugout, demanding a curtain call. But Wood wouldn't come out. The Cubs trailed 2-1 in a game they badly needed to catch the first-place Astros, and for Wood, team goals have always trumped personal achievements.

"I appreciated the fans recognizing me, but we're chasing a pennant, and that's the most important thing on my mind," he said.

Though he may have been supplanted by the gifted Mark Prior as the ace of the Cubs' staff, Wood took his place alongside Prior as the leaders of a team that would go as far as pitching took it. And his resolve symbolized the 2003 Cubs.

Wood pitched well enough in the first half to earn a spot on the All-Star team for the first time, surviving one stretch of six starts in which the Cubs scored seven runs for him. And in big games, he was at his best.

He beat Roger Clemens, his boyhood idol, in a Cubs-Yankees game on June 7 that had jam-packed Wrigley Field rocking to its ancient foundation.

He beat the White Sox on June 29 at

U.S. Cellular Field, averting a sweep.

He threw a two-hit shutout to beat the Florida Marlins 1-0 on July 19, laboring through 130 pitches in Miami's sauna-like conditions.

"I needed Woody to be a stud tonight, and that's what he was," manager Dusty Baker said after that victory. "He's a tough guy, a great competitor and a once-in-a-lifetime talent."

Wood has been a prisoner of expectations since his fifth career start, when he tied a major-league record by striking out 20 Astros in a memorably dominant one-hitter at Wrigley Field. He was 20 years old, and in the wake of all that has transpired since elbow-ligament surgery, an arduous rehabilitation, pitching coaches coming and going and a succession of bad teams, it's easy to lose sight of the fact that Wood is still only 26.

"Kerry's coming to the point in his career where he should be ready to enter his prime, physically and mentally," pitching coach Larry Rothschild said. "There have been times this year when he's looked ready for a breakout year."

Wood finished with a career-high 14 victories and led the National League

with 266 strikeouts. A two-week stretch in July when he gave up grand slams in two successive outings and left a loss to the Dodgers with a sore back after 2 2/3 innings gave rise to some of the old grumbling about inconsistency, but he bounced back with some of his most effective pitching down the stretch. Wood blanked the Mets on three hits with 12 strikeouts Sept. 17 and took a no-hitter into the seventh inning of a 6-0 victory over Cincinnati a week later.

Catcher Damian Miller came to the mound to settle Wood after Wily Mo Pena's cheap infield single cost him the no-hitter, but Wood already was looking ahead to the next batter. There was a playoff race to win.

"I'm pretty happy with where my career is," Wood said. "I'm a much better pitcher than I was when I had the 20-strikeout game. Then I was pretty much flinging it and hoping. Now I have a much better idea what I want to do."

Wood's epiphany may well have come in the All-Star Game on July 15 at U.S. Cellular Field. He worked one inning, facing four batters and striking out two of them.

"I felt like I belonged," he said. ●

In some ways, Kerry Wood is a throw-back: A hard-nosed, hard-throwing pitcher who seems to thrive when the pressure is greatest.

Youth was served as Mark Prior and Kerry Wood became the best young pitching tandem in the National League.

When the team needed him most, Wood was at his best. Here he bears down in the eighth inning of his late-September shutout against the Mets.

Damian Miller was a reliable backstop for Wood. Here he watches as Wood tries to cut down a runner at first in early April.

On the field and off, Kerry Wood was at the center of much of what happened to the Cubs in 2003.

NINTH INNING

THE FINAL PUSH

THE CUBS CAME OUT of the Cardinals series the first week of September with the sort of momentum that made their fans believers. They followed by sweeping a series in Milwaukee against the Brewers. The trouble was that the Houston Astros were winning too. When the Cubs dropped two of three to the

Montreal Expos in San Juan, Puerto Rico–losing one by giving up five runs with two out in the eighth–the Cubs fell out of first place, a game behind Houston.

You could hear the groans across the North Side: Here they go again. But as they had throughout the season, the Cubs came back.

They took two of three from Cincinnati at home but fell two games behind the Astros when Carlos Zambrano lost a 1-0 heartbreaker in the finale. Then they swept the Mets, getting outstanding pitching from Matt Clement in the opener and Mark Prior in the second game. And Kerry Wood pitched one of his best games of the season in the final game of the series, a four-hit, 11-strikeout shutout that brought the team within a half-game of first.

Disappointment again awaited the Cubs and their fans. After a day off, they traveled to Pittsburgh and split a four-game series. But Prior won the last game by striking out 14, and the Cardinals did the Cubs a favor by

knocking off Houston. The team would head to Cincinnati still a half-game behind the Astros.

That didn't last long. Wood, magnificent in his previous outing, was even better against the Reds. He allowed just an infield hit and struck out 12 in a 6-0 victory, while the Astros fell to the Giants. First place belonged to Chicago.

Then came a start that most Cubs fans were dreading. Shawn Estes, who had struggled all season, faced the Reds with the season teetering in the balance. Though he hadn't won a game since July, the veteran left-hander more than rose to the occasion with a four-hit shutout. He thanked manager Dusty Baker for having faith in him.

"That's one of the major reasons I came here, because I knew Dusty would be in my corner," Estes said.

The momentum wouldn't last. Zambrano struggled in the last game of the series and the bullpen imploded in a 9-7 loss. Houston, meanwhile, beat Milwaukee, and with three games left in the season, the Cubs and Astros were tied. "Back to square

one," Baker said.

But the Cubs liked their chances. They were home with Prior, Clement and Wood scheduled to pitch against the Pirates. Even when the opener was rained out, the Cubs won as the woeful Brewers somehow beat the Astros in Houston, putting the Cubs a half-game ahead with three to go, starting with a Saturday doubleheader.

And that was enough. Before a packed house, Prior struck out 10 for his 18th win in Game 1 as the Astros again were losing to the Brewers. And in the nightcap, Sammy Sosa found some vindication for his controversial season, launching a mammoth home run to start the scoring in an eventual 7-2 victory.

When Dave Veres got ex-Cub Jose Hernandez on a double-play ball to end it, a gloomy day turned sunny. Next year was here. The Cubs had their first title since 1989 and were headed to the playoffs.

"History is great," relief pitcher Mike Remlinger said. "But we're here to make some new history." ●

On the final weekend of the season, it was time to pull out all the stops. Here Randall Simon gives it his best shot trying to chase down a foul ball.

Mark Grudzielanek kept the Cubs' opponents on their toes all season, and sometimes, he knocked them off their feet.

Scoreboard watching? Not the Cubs. Pitchers Mark Guthrie and Shawn Estes jokingly took care of that while the Cubs took batting practice in Pittsburgh and the Cardinals and Astros played in St. Louis.

At the end of the
season, Shawn
Estes stood tall as
he threw his best
game of the year –
a shutout against
the Cincinnati
Reds.

Matt Clement didn't want to come out in the eighth inning of the division-clinching game, even though his skipper thanked him for a job well done.

There it goes: Sammy Sosa reached 40 home runs in Game 2 of the doubleheader against the Pirates.

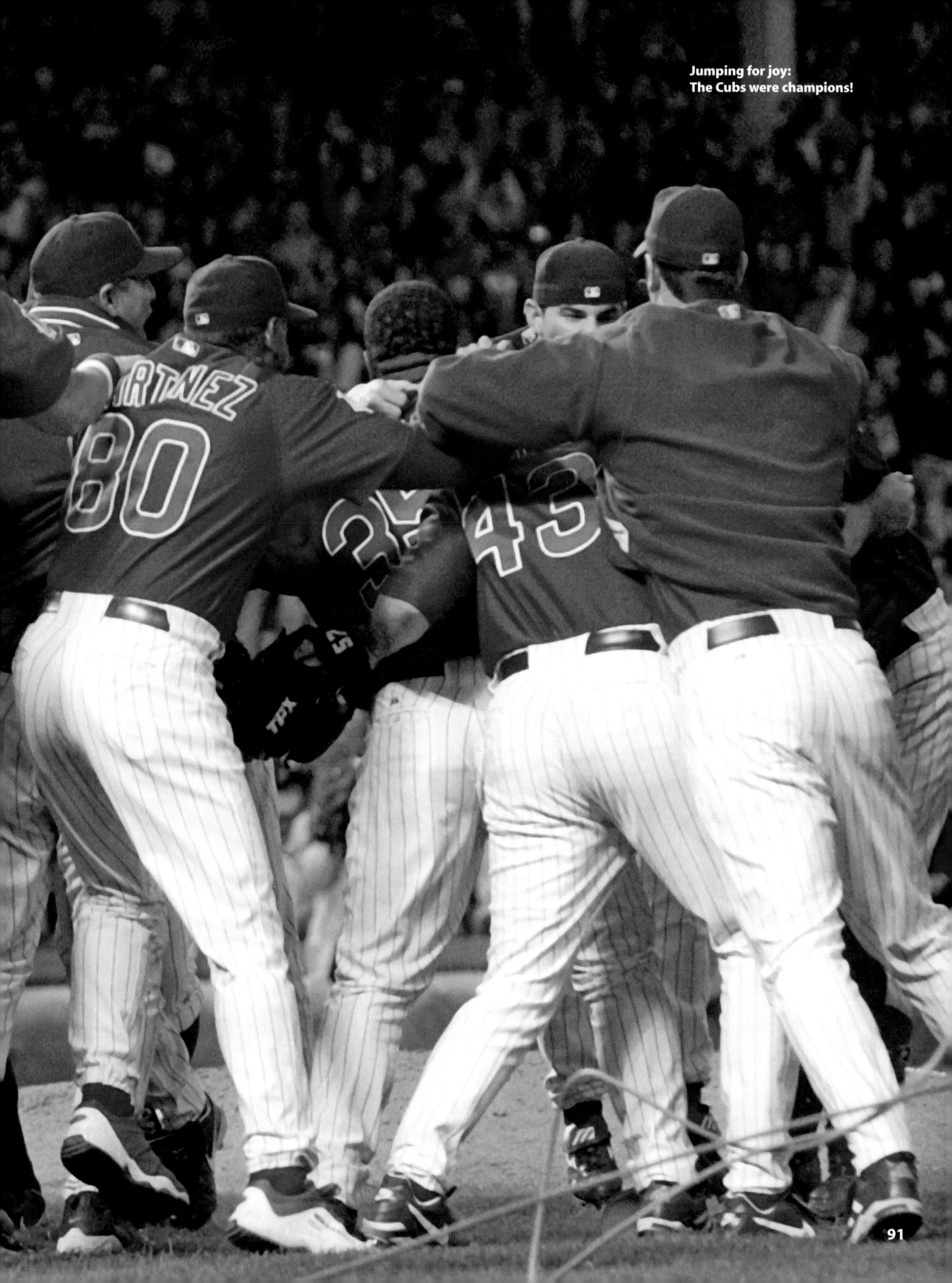

Jumping for joy:
The Cubs were champions!

At the center of everything: Dusty Baker.

Across the city of Chicago, fans celebrated the end of a nightmare and a dream come true.

Sammy Sosa took
a victory lap to
thank the fans.

And he gave them a shower, too.

EXTRA INNINGS

BURNING ATLANTA

THE PROBLEM, BOBBY COX SAID, was that "we couldn't beat their big guys." Cox, the Atlanta Braves' manager, seemed as surprised as the rest of baseball when his National League East champs, who had won 101 games, fell to the Cubs in the NL Division Series. But he certainly pinpointed the reason.

Kerry Wood and Mark Prior beat the Braves three games to two, combining for a 1.48 ERA and 25 strikeouts in 24 1/3 innings against the league's hardest-hitting lineup.

"Any organization in baseball would covet that pitching staff," said Cox, who has had a few good staffs of his own.

Wood got the Cubs started in Game 1, a 4-2 victory in Atlanta. He not only outpitched 21-game winner Russ Ortiz, he broke a 1-1 tie in the sixth inning with a two-run double.

Wood said he was knee-knocking nervous before the game and in the first two innings. "But once I settled down, I was fine," he said. "I liked the way the ball was coming out of my hand."

The Braves came back with a 5-3 victory in Game 2, with Mark DeRosa's two-run double off reliever Dave Veres deciding the game in the eighth inning. The Cubs had a feeling it wasn't their night when Sammy Sosa's first-inning blast to dead center field struck the top of the fence and bounced directly back to Andruw Jones, an apparent three-run homer

converted into an RBI double.

Back in Chicago, Prior faced four-time Cy Young Award winner Greg Maddux in a battle between the Cubs' future and their past. The future won as Prior threw a two-hitter to win 3-1. Randall Simon's two-run first-inning single off Maddux was the game's big hit.

Prior threw 133 pitches and struck out seven in the complete game. He said he "didn't have my best stuff," but the Braves didn't agree.

"The Cubs might have the best pitching staff I've seen in baseball," said Atlanta's Chipper Jones, a nine-year veteran.

With a 2-1 series lead, the Cubs had a chance to close the show in Game 4, but Chipper Jones wouldn't let them. The Atlanta left fielder hit a two-run homer off loser Matt Clement in the third inning and another off Mark Guthrie in the seventh as the Braves won 6-4. Jones had been 1-for-11 through the first three games.

"The difference?" he said. "I finally saw some pitches that weren't 98 m.p.h. on the black."

The game ended in high drama, a "powder river" confrontation between Sosa and Braves closer John Smoltz. Sosa drove Smoltz's 3-2 pitch to deep center, but Andruw Jones caught it at the warning track, about eight feet shy of a game-tying homer.

Some Cubs fans feared the worst as they headed back to Atlanta for Game 5, but Wood had matters under control. He continued the best run of his career with eight innings of three-hit work, Joe Borowski worked a perfect ninth for his second save of the series, and Alex Gonzaelez and Aramis Ramirez slugged homers as the Cubs won 5-1 to win their first postseason series since 1908.

"Our fans deserve this," Prior said, alluding not only to the record crowds that packed Wrigley Field all season but to the thousands who accompanied the Cubs to Atlanta and joined in the celebration after Game 5 at Turner Field.

"Chicago people are really into this," Cubs manager Dusty Baker said. "But I think we've given them something they can get into." ●

Marcus Giles collided with Mark Prior back in July, but Moises Alou couldn't upset him as he turned a double play in the playoffs.

AVERAGE
.333

B
0

Kerry Wood got it done with his
arm and his bat in Game 1,
driving in two runs with a
booming double before stop-
ping to catch a breather.

Kenny Lofton made a spectacular catch in Game 5 against the Braves, but the umpires didn't see it that way.

Mark Prior showed that the Cubs' future might be brighter than their past as he outdueled former Chicago ace Greg Maddux in Game 3.

Eric Karros couldn't hold onto the ball when Atlanta's Robert Fick hooked his glove hand during Game 4, but Fick was called out for interference anyway.

After a masterpiece on the mound, Kerry Wood celebrated his Game 5 victory with Chicago fans who had traveled to watch their team.

FIVE OUTS AWAY

THE DREAM THAT began with a simple question from Dusty Baker—"Why not us?"—would end with a gentle fly ball off the bat of Paul Bako that nestled in the glove of Florida Marlins left-fielder Jeff Conine. ❧ But for many, the dream had begun to unravel the night before, when another gentle fly ball floated toward

the seats down the left-field line, destined to land with a crunching thud in the nightmares of Cubs fans.

It didn't start so badly. Though the Cubs lost Game 1 of the National League Championship Series 9-8, they got some heroics from Sammy Sosa, who hit a two-run homer with two outs in the ninth to force extra innings. "We'll be all right," Baker said. "Sammy hit a huge, clutch home run, some other guys swung the bats well and we're coming back with our horses."

That would be Mark Prior and Kerry Wood, and the next night Prior coasted to a 12-3 victory at Wrigley Field. Sosa hit his second home run of the NLCS, a 495-foot blast that bounced off the camera shed in the center-field bleachers. Alex Gonzalez added two home runs and Aramis Ramirez one.

"This is a great feeling," Sosa said. "Nobody thought we'd be in this position today, but here we are."

Then the series shifted to Miami, where Wood struggled but pitched well enough to keep the Cubs in Game 3, and just long enough to allow two unlikely heroes, Doug Glanville and Randall Simon, to take center stage. In the eighth, Simon powered a two-run homer to erase Florida's 3-2 lead. Glanville, pinch-hitting in the 11th, smacked a triple to score Kenny Lofton with the game-winning run as the Cubs won 5-4.

Game 4 was another laugher, an 8-3 victory sparked by Ramirez's first-inning grand slam off rookie sensation Dontrelle Willis. The Cubs were within a victory of their first World Series in 58 years and were ready to finish off the Marlins in Miami.

But Florida's Josh Beckett, a baby-faced Texan who threw as hard as Wood and Prior, cooled the Cubs in Game 5 with a two-hit 4-0 shutout. The Cubs never got a runner past second, but they felt confident as they headed back to Chicago with Prior and Wood rested and ready.

Instead, the unthinkable happened. With the Cubs leading 3-0 in the eighth inning of Game 6 and Prior on the mound, a fan down the left-field line tried to catch a foul ball that Moises Alou appeared ready to grab for the second out. The ball glanced off the fan's hand and bounced free. The crowd of 39,577 gasped; the Cubs, who were five outs from victory, seemed to sag. Momentum teetered on a knife's edge, then swung inexorably toward Florida. Before the inning ended, the Cubs had coughed up eight runs. They lost 8-3.

The following night, 39,574 packed Wrigley for the decisive Game 7. Wood gave up three runs in the first inning but tied it in the second with a two-run home run of his own. Alou added another two-run homer in the third to put the Cubs up 5-3.

Yet the Marlins came back again, scoring six runs over the fifth, sixth and seventh innings and knocking Wood out of the box. Beckett came out of the bullpen on two days' rest and shut down the Cubs one last time. Final score: 9-6, Marlins.

"Is it disappointing?" Baker asked. "Yeah, it's disappointing because we wanted to go to the World Series. But life is full of disappointments sometimes, and you've got to build something for the future."

The dream—and Chicago—would wait until next year. Again. ●

The mitt hit the fan: Moises Alou thought he was going to catch this foul for the second out in the eighth inning of Game 6. But then a fan reached out and the ball fell into Cubs lore.

The city and the stadium were set aglow
at the prospect of a National League
championship pennant -- and a World
Series -- coming to Chicago.

Two outs, one on, the bottom of the ninth and Sammy Sosa at bat in Game 1. With one swing, the fans' prayers were answered and the Cubs were all tied up—and the roller-coaster ride of emotions kept going for two more innings.

The Cubs nearly gave away Game 3, but Luis Castillo was caught off second and wound up in a rundown. When it was over, the Cubs had a 3-1 series lead.

Randall Simon was the man of the hour after he put the Cubs on top with a two-run home run in Game 3.

Aramis Ramirez was the focus of attention for a traveling band of Cubs fans after his two-homer, six-RBI performance in Game 4.

Sam Sianis, nephew of the man who first leveled the Billy Goat curse on the Cubs, tried to reverse the team's fortunes.

The firefighters across Waveland Avenue couldn't see the action but they could hear the roar.

Mark Prior and everyone else wore their heart on their sleeve as the fateful pop foul drifted toward the left-field stands in the eighth inning of Game 6.

No one could bear to watch the crazy eighth inning of Game 6, including these fans at a Berwyn sports bar.

Paul Bako couldn't bear to watch as Miguel Cabrera scored what turned out to be the winning run in Game 6.

After falling behind 3 games to 1, the Florida Marlins rallied, won three games in a row and became the 2003 National League champions.

Kerry Wood pitched his heart out and slugged a two-run home run in Game 7 of the NLCS, but in the end, neither he nor his teammates could watch the season come to an end.

Outside the ballpark, fans watched heartbroken as the last outs were made in the 2003 season—one they would never forget.

2003 PLAYOFF ROSTER

THE PITCHERS

GS	CG	Sv	BS	Hld	P/GS	BAA	WHIP	ERA
Games started	Complete games	Saves	Blown saves	Holds	Pitches per game started	Batters average against	Walks+hits per inning pitched	Earned run average

Matt Clement
 # 30

Position: Starting pitcher
Bats: R Throws: R
Age: 29 H: 6-3 W: 210
Experience: 6 years

	G	GS	CG	IP	H	R	ER	HR	BB	SO	W	L	Sv	P/GS	BAA	WHIP	ERA
2003	32	32	2	201.2	169	100	92	22	79	171	14	12	0	98.4	.227	1.23	4.11
Career	164	162	5	975.1	902	531	483	95	467	838	60	62	0	97.6	.246	1.40	4.46

At 29, he established himself as a credible starter with career-high 14 victories, following up his breakthrough 2002 campaign. Won the division clincher vs. Pittsburgh on Sept. 27. Worked six or more innings in 23 of his 32 starts. Cubs had an 18-14 record in those starts.

Juan Cruz
 # 51

Position: Starting pitcher
Bats: R Throws: R
Age: 24 H: 6-2 W: 165
Experience: 3 years

	G	GS	CG	IP	H	R	ER	HR	BB	SO	W	L	Sv	P/GS	BAA	WHIP	ERA
2003	25	6	0	61.0	66	44	41	7	28	65	2	7	0	95.3	.275	1.54	6.05
Career	78	23	0	203.0	190	116	100	22	104	185	8	19	1	89.6	.252	1.45	4.43

Slender young right-hander didn't get many chances to pitch because the starting rotation mostly avoided injury. Cubs went 3-3 in his six starts. Beat Milwaukee on Sept. 5 for his first big-league win as a starter since May 2002.

Mark Prior
 # 22

Position: Starting pitcher
Bats: R Throws: R
Age: 23 H: 6-5 W: 230
Experience: 2 years

	G	GS	CG	IP	H	R	ER	HR	BB	SO	W	L	Sv	P/GS	BAA	WHIP	ERA
2003	30	30	3	211.1	183	67	57	15	50	245	18	6	0	113.4	.231	1.10	2.43
Career	49	49	4	328.0	281	112	100	29	88	392	24	12	0	110.9	.229	1.13	2.74

Candidate for the Cy Young Award in his first full big league season. Second in the NL in wins, second in strikeouts and third in ERA despite missing three weeks with a bruised shoulder. Went 10-1 after his return from disabled list and beat Braves and Marlins once each in the playoffs.

Kerry Wood
 # 34

Position: Starting pitcher
Bats: R Throws: R
Age: 26 H: 6-5 W: 225
Experience: 5 years

	G	GS	CG	IP	H	R	ER	HR	BB	SO	W	L	Sv	P/GS	BAA	WHIP	ERA
2003	32	32	4	211.0	152	77	75	24	100	266	14	11	0	110.8	.203	1.19	3.20
Career	142	142	11	902.2	677	385	363	93	461	1065	59	41	0	106.9	.209	1.26	3.62

Long-awaited breakout year. Career high in wins, led league in strikeouts and was eighth in ERA as opponents hit just .203 against him. Beat boyhood idol Roger Clemens at Wrigley on June 7. Pitched two shutouts, was 3-1 with an 0.84 ERA in last six starts and beat Braves twice in playoffs.

Carlos Zambrano
 # 38

Position: Starting pitcher
Bats: B Throws: R
Age: 22 H: 6-5 W: 245
Experience: 5 years

	G	GS	CG	IP	H	R	ER	HR	BB	SO	W	L	Sv	P/GS	BAA	WHIP	ERA
2003	32	32	3	214.0	188	88	74	9	94	168	13	11	0	106.7	.239	1.32	3.11
Career	70	49	3	330.0	293	154	131	20	165	265	18	21	0	103.5	.241	1.39	3.57

Established himself as solid No. 3 starter with strong second half, going 7-3 with a 2.51 ERA and three complete games after All-Star break. Seventh in NL in ERA and eighth in innings pitched. Beat Houston 5-3 on July 25, retiring 24 of 26 batters and tying game with two-run homer.

Antonio Alfonseca
 # 57

Position: Relief pitcher
Bats: R Throws: R
Age: 31 H: 6-5 W: 250
Experience: 7 years

	G	GS	IP	H	R	ER	HR	BB	SO	W	L	Hld	Sv	BS	BAA	WHIP	ERA
2003	60	0	66.1	76	43	43	7	27	51	3	1	9	0	4	.290	1.55	5.83
Career	400	0	446.1	489	216	204	42	174	310	23	30	23	121	35	.282	1.49	4.11

Spring-training injury cost him his closer's role, and he was unable to regain it because Joe Borowski was so effective. Pitched in seven straight games from May 5-May 13 and won back-to-back games on Sept. 12 and 13.

Joe Borowski
 # 48

Position: Relief pitcher
Bats: R Throws: R
Age: 32 H: 6-2 W: 225
Experience: 7 years

	G	GS	IP	H	R	ER	HR	BB	SO	W	L	Hld	Sv	BS	BAA	WHIP	ERA
2003	68	0	68.1	53	23	20	5	19	66	2	2	1	33	4	.207	1.05	2.63
Career	199	1	234.2	221	96	89	22	92	197	11	14	16	35	8	.250	1.33	3.41

Journeyman middle reliever seized the closer's job in spring training and wouldn't let it go, converting 33 of 37 save opportunities with a career-best 2.63 ERA. Was 14 for 14 in saves since Aug. 1 on, allowing one earned run in 19 innings over his last 18 games. Fourteen of his saves came in one-run games.

Kyle Farnsworth
 # 44

Position: Relief pitcher
Bats: R Throws: R
Age: 27 H: 6-4 W: 235
Experience: 5 years

	G	GS	IP	H	R	ER	HR	BB	SO	W	L	Hld	Sv	BS	BAA	WHIP	ERA
2003	77	0	76.1	53	31	28	6	36	92	3	2	19	0	3	.196	1.17	3.30
Career	271	26	412.0	401	242	219	65	191	389	18	32	55	4	15	.253	1.44	4.78

Best remembered for his takedown of the Reds' Paul Wilson in a game at Cincinnati on June 19, but he was a dependable right-handed set-up man who struck out 92 batters in 76 1/3 innings. Unscored on in 13 of his last 14 games. Opponents batted just .196 against him.

Mark Guthrie
 # 31

Position: Relief pitcher

Bats: R Throws: L

Age: 38 H: 6-4 W: 215

Experience: 15 years

	G	GS	IP	H	R	ER	HR	BB	SO	W	L	Hld	Sv	BS	BAA	WHIP	ERA
2003	65	0	42.2	40	14	13	6	22	24	2	3	10	0	1	.260	1.45	2.74
Career	765	43	978.2	989	489	440	101	381	778	51	54	155	14	21	.266	1.40	4.05

"Situational" lefty was an experienced bullpen presence in his second tour with the Cubs, compiling a 2.74 ERA in 65 regular-season appearances. Stranded 36 of the 50 baserunners he inherited and was unscored on in 24 games from June 20-Aug. 14.

Mike Remlinger
 # 37

Position: Relief pitcher

Bats: L Throws: L

Age: 37 H: 6-1 W: 215

Experience: 11 years

	G	GS	IP	H	R	ER	HR	BB	SO	W	L	Hld	Sv	BS	BAA	WHIP	ERA
2003	73	0	69.0	54	30	28	11	39	83	6	5	17	0	1	.211	1.35	3.65
Career	512	59	780.1	678	352	328	91	388	765	50	46	138	16	17	.235	1.37	3.78

Lefty set-up man gave the Cubs dependable late-game savvy. Struck out 83 in 69 innings. Opponents hit .211 against him, right-handers just .180. Bases-loaded strikeout of Yankees' Jason Giambi in "Wood-Clemens game" a season highlight.

Dave Veres
 # 43

Position: Relief pitcher

Bats: R Throws: R

Age: 36 H: 6-2 W: 225

Experience: 10 years

	G	GS	IP	H	R	ER	HR	BB	SO	W	L	Hld	Sv	BS	BAA	WHIP	ERA
2003	31	0	32.2	36	17	17	4	5	26	2	1	4	1	1	.290	1.26	4.68
Career	605	0	694.0	661	287	265	78	257	617	36	35	84	95	36	.253	1.32	3.44

Shoulder injury limited him to 31 games, but Dusty Baker was not afraid to use the veteran in game-on-the-line situations. Induced the game-ending, double-play grounder from Pittsburgh's Jose Hernandez in the division-clincher on Sept. 27.

THE HITTERS

CS	BA	OBP	SLG	OPS
Caught stealing	Batting average	On-base percentage	Slugging percentage	On-base percentage + slugging percentage

Paul Bako
 # 9

Position: Catcher

Bats: L Throws: R

Age: 31 H: 6-2 W: 215

Experience: 6 years

	G	AB	R	H	2B	3B	HR	RBI	BB	SO	SB	CS	BA	OBP	SLG	OPS
2003	70	188	19	43	13	3	0	17	22	0	0	1	.229	.311	.330	.641
Career	468	1300	119	315	67	8	13	119	138	3	3	5	.242	.314	.336	.650

Left-handed complement to Miller had a six-RBI game at Cincinnati on April 5 and hit .272 over the season's final 28 games. Threw out Juan Pierre and Luis Castillo as they attempted to steal second in the sixth inning of the Cubs' 1-0 victory at Florida on July 19.

Damian Miller
 # 27

Position: Catcher

Bats: R Throws: R

Age: 33 H: 6-3 W: 220

Experience: 7 years

	G	AB	R	H	2B	3B	HR	RBI	BB	SO	SB	CS	BA	OBP	SLG	OPS
2003	114	352	34	82	19	1	9	36	39	91	1	0	.233	.310	.369	.680
Career	606	1883	219	494	118	3	59	243	180	466	4	3	.262	.329	.422	.751

Veteran was a steady defensive presence behind the plate, discouraging would-be base-stealers with his throwing and skillfully handling a young pitching staff. Cubs pitchers had a 3.88 ERA when he caught, and he made just three errors.

Alex Gonzalez
 # 8

Position: Shortstop

Bats: R Throws: R

Age: 30 H: 6-0 W: 200

Experience: 10 years

	G	AB	R	H	2B	3B	HR	RBI	BB	SO	SB	CS	BA	OBP	SLG	OPS
2003	152	536	71	122	37	0	20	59	47	123	3	3	.228	.295	.409	.704
Career	1184	4307	536	1047	236	25	121	470	350	1017	93	45	.243	.304	.394	.698

Hit a career-high 20 homers, three of them game-winners, but made his biggest contribution defensively with only 10 errors in 152 games. His .984 fielding percentage led NL shortstops. Had a two-homer game at San Francisco on May 1, a homer in Game 5 of the division series and three in the NLCS.

Mark Grudzielanek
 # 11

Position: Second base

Bats: R Throws: R

Age: 33 H: 6-1 W: 190

Experience: 9 years

	G	AB	R	H	2B	3B	HR	RBI	BB	SO	SB	CS	BA	OBP	SLG	OPS
2003	121	481	73	151	38	1	3	38	30	64	6	2	.314	.366	.416	.782
Career	1218	4825	649	1377	261	25	60	420	245	661	116	40	.285	.329	.387	.716

The Cubs' unsung hero, if not their MVP. Won the second-base job from Bobby Hill in spring training and had his best year since 1999, batting .314 with a team-high 38 doubles despite missing nearly a month with a fractured hand. Hit .359 in 24 September games with 16 RBIs and was an inspiration with his all-out effort.

Eric Karros
 # 32

Position: First base

Bats: R Throws: R

Age: 35 H: 6-4 W: 220

Experience: 13 years

	G	AB	R	H	2B	3B	HR	RBI	BB	SO	SB	CS	BA	OBP	SLG	OPS
2003	114	336	37	96	16	1	12	40	28	46	1	1	.286	.340	.446	.786
Career	1715	6338	789	1704	318	11	282	1016	545	1151	58	30	.269	.326	.456	.782

Right-handed half of the first-base platoon produced 12 homers and 40 RBIs in 336 at-bats. Won the "Wood-Clemens" game with a three-run homer against the Yankees on June 7. Went back-to-back with Moises Alou to beat the Reds 4-3 on June 16, and hit two solo homers in Game 4 of the Division Series.

Ramon Martinez
 # 6

Position: Catcher

Bats: R **Throws:** R

Age: 30 **H:** 6-1 **W:** 195

Experience: 6 years

	G	AB	R	H	2B	3B	HR	RBI	BB	SO	SB	CS	BA	OBP	SLG	OPS
2003	108	293	30	83	16	1	3	34	24	50	0	1	.283	.333	.375	.709
Career	476	1217	159	332	64	8	23	140	109	169	7	7	.273	.334	.395	.730

Versatile utilityman who played for Dusty Baker in San Francisco was used at all four infield positions and was a productive right-handed bat off the bench. Had a four-hit game at Houston on May 23. Started 33 games at second base, mostly while Mark Grudzielanek was hurt, and 18 at shortstop. Batted .285 as a starter.

Aramis Ramirez
 # 16

Position: Third base

Bats: R **Throws:** R

Age: 25 **H:** 6-1 **W:** 212

Experience: 6 years

	G	AB	R	H	2B	3B	HR	RBI	BB	SO	SB	CS	BA	OBP	SLG	OPS
2003	159	607	75	165	32	2	27	106	42	99	2	2	.272	.324	.465	.788
Career	622	2293	253	602	124	6	91	355	145	411	9	7	.263	.312	.441	.753

Another gift from Pittsburgh who solved a longstanding problem at third base. Was the Cubs' most productive hitter down the stretch, with five homers and 11 RBI in the final 12 games. In all, he hit 15 homers and drove in 39 runs in 63 games with the Cubs, and he hit a grand slam in the NLCS.

Randall Simon
 # 35

Position: First base

Bats: L **Throws:** L

Age: 28 **H:** 6-0 **W:** 240

Experience: 6 years

	G	AB	R	H	2B	3B	HR	RBI	BB	SO	SB	CS	BA	OBP	SLG	OPS
2003	151	565	83	158	35	1	22	91	63	67	3	1	.280	.357	.462	.819
Career	1464	5287	829	1588	318	31	239	986	986	706	92	34	.300	.367	.508	.875

Late-season acquisition from Pittsburgh not only provided capable defense and a potent left-handed bat, he livened up the clubhouse with his personality. Batted .282 with six homers and 21 RBI in 33 games with the Cubs and delivered the two-run single that beat Greg Maddux in Game 3 of the division playoffs.

Moises Alou
 # 18

Position: Left field

Bats: R **Throws:** R

Age: 37 **H:** 6-3 **W:** 220

Experience: 12 years

	G	AB	R	H	2B	3B	HR	RBI	BB	SO	SB	CS	BA	OBP	SLG	OPS
2003	151	565	83	158	35	1	22	91	63	67	3	1	.280	.357	.462	.819
Career	1464	5287	829	1588	318	31	239	986	556	706	92	34	.300	.367	.508	.875

Rebounded from 2002 and was Cubs' most consistent RBI man for much the season. Had a 5-for-5, four-RBI game in a Sept. 7 win over St. Louis. Batted .359 against the Cardinals with seven homers and 16 RBI, and .352 against Houston with three homers.

Doug Glanville
 # 4

Position: Center field

Bats: R **Throws:** R

Age: 33 **H:** 6-2 **W:** 174

Experience: 8 years

	G	AB	R	H	2B	3B	HR	RBI	BB	SO	SB	CS	BA	OBP	SLG	OPS
2003	52	195	22	53	5	0	4	14	6	25	4	0	.272	.294	.359	.653
Career	1028	3802	532	1066	165	31	57	319	200	481	160	36	.280	.318	.385	.703

Late-season acquisition got only 51 at-bats after coming over from Texas on July 30. Led off Sept. 17 Mets game with a home run off Al Leiter, and Kerry Wood went on to pitch a shutout.

Tom Goodwin
 # 24

Position: Center field

Bats: L **Throws:** R

Age: 35 **H:** 6-0 **W:** 185

Experience: 13 years

	G	AB	R	H	2B	3B	HR	RBI	BB	SO	SB	CS	BA	OBP	SLG	OPS
2003	87	171	26	49	10	0	1	12	11	33	19	5	.287	.328	.363	.690
Career	1211	3741	625	1008	117	39	24	281	357	638	364	118	.269	.334	.341	.675

Speedy outfielder was a useful spare part, hitting .287 with 26 runs scored and 19 stolen bases in 87 games. Won the May 29 Pittsburgh game with a ninth-inning home run and had five hits and scored four runs in a victory over the Braves at Atlanta on July 21.

Kenny Lofton
 # 7

Position: Center field

Bats: L **Throws:** L

Age: 36 **H:** 6-0 **W:** 180

Experience: 13 years

	G	AB	R	H	2B	3B	HR	RBI	BB	SO	SB	CS	BA	OBP	SLG	OPS
2003	140	547	97	162	32	8	12	46	46	51	30	9	.296	.352	.450	.801
Career	1645	6518	1245	1943	318	86	115	648	781	855	538	142	.298	.373	.426	.799

Rode to the rescue for Dusty Baker again, as he did in San Francisco last year. Came over from Pittsburgh after Patterson was injured and energized the lineup, hitting .327, scoring 39 runs and stealing 12 bases in 56 games. His teams have reached the playoffs in eight consecutive seasons.

Troy O'Leary
 # 25

Position: Left field

Bats: L **Throws:** L

Age: 34 **H:** 6-0 **W:** 205

Experience: 11 years

	G	AB	R	H	2B	3B	HR	RBI	BB	SO	SB	CS	BA	OBP	SLG	OPS
2003	93	174	18	38	9	0	5	28	14	31	3	0	.218	.275	.356	.631
Career	1198	4010	547	1100	234	40	127	591	334	661	17	22	.274	.332	.448	.780

The Cubs' most productive left-handed bat off the bench, driving in 28 runs in just 174 at-bats. Homered twice and drove in seven runs as the starting right fielder during Sammy Sosa's suspension. Hit his third career grand slam at Toronto on June 15.

Sammy Sosa
 # 21

Position: Right field

Bats: R **Throws:** R

Age: 34 **H:** 6-0 **W:** 220

Experience: 15 years

	G	AB	R	H	2B	3B	HR	RBI	BB	SO	SB	CS	BA	OBP	SLG	OPS
2003	137	517	99	144	22	0	40	103	62	143	0	1	.297	.358	.553	.911
Career	2102	7543	1314	2099	319	43	539	1450	800	1977	233	106	.278	.349	.546	.895

Despite injuries and a suspension for using a corked bat, he had another productive season, reaching 40 homers for the sixth straight year and 100 RBI for the ninth. Hit 13 homers in July and had five two-homer games. His 464 homers since 1994 are the most ever over a 10-year period.

2003 POSTSEASON

PLAYER STATS

	G	GS	IP	H	R	ER	HR	BB	SO	W	L	Sv	WHIP	ERA
Matt Clement	2	2	12.1	13	7	7	1	6	6	1	1	0	1.54	5.11
Juan Cruz	1	0	1.0	0	0	0	0	1	2	0	0	0	1.00	0.00
Mark Prior	3	3	23.1	16	9	6	2	9	18	2	1	0	1.07	2.31
Kerry Wood	4	4	27.2	21	13	13	2	14	31	2	1	0	1.27	4.23
Carlos Zambrano	3	3	16.2	25	11	10	4	5	12	0	1	0	1.80	5.40

	G	GS	IP	H	R	ER	HR	BB	SO	W	L	Sv	WHIP	ERA
Antonio Alfonseca	4	0	3.1	3	0	0	0	2	0	0	0	0	1.50	0.00
Joe Borowski	5	0	7.2	6	2	1	0	3	6	1	0	1	1.17	1.17
Kyle Farnsworth	8	0	8.0	7	6	6	0	3	9	0	0	0	1.25	6.75
Mark Guthrie	3	0	1.2	3	3	3	2	1	0	0	1	0	2.40	16.20
Mike Remlinger	7	0	4	3	1	1	1	2	3	0	0	1	1.25	2.25
Dave Veres	5	0	4.1	6	3	3	1	3	0	0	1	0	2.08	6.23

	AB	R	H	2B	3B	HR	RBI	BB	SO	SB	CS	BA
Paul Bako	20	4	4	1	0	0	2	3	9	0	0	.200
Damian Miller	21	0	3	2	0	0	2	4	7	0	0	.143
Alex Gonzalez	40	6	11	2	0	4	8	4	10	0	1	.275
Mark Grudzielanek	50	4	9	1	1	0	3	3	9	0	0	.180
Eric Karros	29	6	9	0	0	2	2	2	6	0	0	.310
Ramon Martinez	8	0	0	0	0	0	0	0	3	0	0	.000
Aramis Ramirez	44	6	11	1	1	4	10	7	8	0	0	.250
Randall Simon	24	4	8	3	0	1	6	0	5	0	0	.333
Moises Alou	49	7	19	2	0	2	8	3	5	1	0	.388
Doug Glanville	2	1	1	0	1	0	1	0	0	0	0	.500
Tom Goodwin	5	1	2	1	1	0	2	0	3	0	0	.400
Kenny Lofton	52	11	16	2	0	0	3	5	6	4	1	.308
Troy O'Leary	4	1	1	0	0	1	1	0	0	0	0	.250
Sammy Sosa	42	8	11	2	0	2	7	12	13	1	0	.262

POSTSEASON GAMES

GAME	DATE	OPPONENT	SCORE	WIN	LOSS	THE SKINNY
1.	9/30	@Atlanta	4-2	●		Wood held the Braves to two hits, struck out 11—and hit two-run double that put Cubs ahead.
2.	10/1	@Atlanta	5-3		●	Reserve infielder Mark DeRosa had game-winning double in eighth as the Braves evened the series.
3.	10/3	Atlanta	3-1	●		Prior threw a two-hitter to outduel Maddux as Simon and Ramirez provided timely offense.
4.	10/4	Atlanta	6-4		●	Overcoming Karros' two home runs, Braves forced a deciding game.
5.	10/5	@Atlanta	5-1	●		Wood continued strong playoffs scattering five hits over eight as Ramirez and Gonzalez homered.
6.	10/7	Florida	9-8 (11)		●	Sosa hit a game-tying home run in the ninth, but Lowell won it with a pinch HR in 11th.
7.	10/8	Florida	12-3	●		An easy game for Prior, and the Cubs batters kept slugging: Two HR for Gonzalez.
8.	10/10	@Florida	5-4 (11)	●		Randall Simon and Doug Glanville were the unlikely heroes; Glanville's triple won it.
9.	10/11	@Florida	8-3	●		Aramis Ramirez belted an early grand slam and another home run, drove in 6 runs.
10.	10/12	@Florida	4-0		●	Josh Beckett proved Wood and Prior weren't the only great young pitchers, allowing just 2 hits.
11.	10/14	Florida	8-3		●	Crazy 8th inning was costly: Cubs blew a 3-0 lead just five outs away from the World Series.
12.	10/15	Florida	9-6		●	Home runs by Wood, Alou, O'Leary weren't enough as storybook season came to an end.

2003 REGULAR SEASON

GAME	DATE	OPPONENT	SCORE	WIN	LOSS	THE SKINNY
1.	3/31	@NY Mets	15-2	●		Corey Patterson hit two home runs and had seven RBI in Dusty Baker's Cubs debut.
2.	4/2	@NY Mets	4-1		●	Stuck at 499 career HRs, Sammy Sosa hopped, skipped and jumped but came up short.
3.	4/3	@NY Mets	6-3	●		Sosa's two singles drove in three. Moises Alou had three RBI. Mark Prior was the winner.
4.	4/4	@Cincinnati	10-9		●	500th homer for Sosa as Cubs overcame 7-0 deficit but lost in ninth on Barry Larkin's RBI single.
5.	4/5	@Cincinnati	9-7	●		Paul Bako (career-high six RBI) hit a bases-loaded triple as Ken Griffey Jr. injured himself.
6.	4/6	@Cincinnati	5-4		●	Cubs led 4-0 but lost on Sean Casey's solo homer in the eighth inning off Mark Guthrie.
7.	4/8	Montreal	6-1	●		After Monday's snowout, Baker won home opener behind Matt Clement (7 1/3 innings, 1 ER).
8.	4/9	Montreal	3-0	●		Prior (2-0) struck out 12, walked none and yielded just four hits in complete-game shutout.
9.	4/10	Montreal	7-1		●	Expos starter Tony Armas Jr. responded to Prior's outing with career-high 11 strikeouts.
10.	4/11	Pittsburgh	3-2		●	Aramis Ramirez went 2-for-3 with an RBI as Pirates jumped out to 3-0 lead after 3 1/2 innings.
11.	4/12	Pittsburgh	4-0	●		Kerry Wood struck out 13, allowing just three hits over 8 innings. Joe Borowski notched the save.
12.	4/13	Pittsburgh	4-3	●		Cubs took lead in eighth with two runs: Patterson's RBI single and Troy O'Leary's sac fly.
13.	4/14	Cincinnati	11-3		●	Prior's 0.60 ERA took a pounding as he gave up 5 runs in 6 innings. Cubs committed three errors.
14.	4/15	Cincinnati	11-1	●		HRs for Sosa, Mark Bellhorn and Hee Seop Choi. Shawn Estes threw no-hit ball through five.
15.	4/16	Cincinnati	10-4	●		Sosa hit three-run homer in first inning. Damian Miller, Choi and Alou also homered.
16.	4/17	Cincinnati	16-3	●		Third straight 10-run outing. HRs for Wood, Choi, Mark Grudzielanek and Sosa (his 503rd).
17.	4/18	@Pittsburgh	7-2	●		Cubs scored four in first. Clement, Kyle Farnsworth and Borowski yielded just three hits.
18.	4/19	@Pittsburgh	6-1, (10)	●		Grudzielanek knocked in go-ahead run in five-run 10th. Prior (3-1) pitched nine innings.
19.	4/20	@Pittsburgh	8-2		●	Sosa's helmet shattered by pitch from Salomon Torres. Estes allowed five runs in three innings.
20.	4/22	San Diego	7-2	●		Patterson had three RBI and HR. Miller added three RBI. Carlos Zambrano (3-1) the winner.
21.	4/23	San Diego	2-0		●	Wood struck out 11, but Padres' Adam Eaton whiffed 12 Cubs through seven innings.
22.	4/24	San Diego	2-1		●	Oliver Perez, winless in four starts, pitched Padres to their second win on road this season.
23.	4/25	@Colorado	11-7	●		Prior not only picked up victory, but he hit his first major-league home run and had four RBI.
24.	4/26	@Colorado	8-5		●	Estes gave up seven runs on 12 hits through two innings. Rockies led 8-2 after fourth.
25.	4/27	@Colorado	6-3		●	Jay Payton's two-out RBI infield single in seventh inning gave Rockies lead for good.
26.	4/29	@San Francisco	4-2	●		Alou, playing against his father, homered and drove in two runs in Baker's return to Frisco.
27.	4/30	@San Francisco	5-0		●	Giants starter Jason Schmidt struck out 12, yielded just three hits in complete-game victory.
28.	5/1	@San Francisco	5-1 (10)	●		Alex Gonzalez hit three-run homer in the 10th inning. Prior plunked Barry Bonds in third.
29.	5/2	Colorado	7-4	●		Bellhorn went 2-for-2 with three RBI, while Estes picked up the win along with an RBI.
30.	5/3	Colorado	6-4		●	Preston Wilson's two-run, eighth-inning home run gave the Rockies the lead for good.
31.	5/4	Colorado	5-4, (10)	●		Gonzalez did it again, hitting a game-winning solo homer in the 10th inning off Steve Reed.
32.	5/5	Milwaukee	5-3		●	Starter Ben Sheets improved to 6-0 lifetime vs. the Cubs.
33.	5/6	Milwaukee	9-6		●	Bullpen let down Prior as Brewers overcame three-run deficit with six runs in final two innings.
34.	5/7	Milwaukee	2-1	●		Estes three-hit Brewers through seven innings, while Borowski recorded sixth save.
35.	5/9	St. Louis	6-3		●	St. Louis' Fernando Vina hit a second-inning grand slam. Matt Morris improved to 4-2.
36.	5/10	St. Louis	3-2, (10)	●		Cards tied it in ninth. Gonzalez homered in 10th for victory. Sosa placed on DL (right toe).
37.	5/12	@Milwaukee	11-5	●		Alou and Grudzielanek had four hits apiece as Cubs rapped season-high 19 hits.
38.	5/13	@Milwaukee	7-2	●		Estes won third straight decision and first on the road. Choi and Patterson had 2 RBI apiece.
39.	5/14	@Milwaukee	6-1	●		Zambrano allowed three hits over eight innings, while O'Leary ripped three-run homer.
40.	5/15	@Milwaukee	4-2, (17)	●		Patterson's two-run HR off Brooks Kieschnick ended 17-inning affair and completed sweep.
41.	5/16	@St. Louis	7-4		●	With bullpen tired from previous day, Baker had Clement bat in 6th down a run with runners on.
42.	5/17	@St. Louis	2-1	●		Bellhorn's ninth-inning leadoff home run off Steve Kline broke 1-1 tie. Borowski's 7th save.
43.	5/18	@St. Louis	6-3		●	Cards scored three in seventh as Cubs dropped to 4-22 in last 26 at Busch Stadium.
44.	5/19	@St. Louis	2-0		●	Morris (5-3) pitched a complete game, struck out eight and allowed just four hits.
45.	5/21	@Pittsburgh	5-2		●	Jack Wilson and Brian Giles homered in the span of five pitches against Wood in the sixth.
46.	5/22	@Pittsburgh	3-2	●		Tom Goodwin's tie-breaking solo home run in the top of the ninth was the difference.
47.	5/23	@Houston	7-5		●	Prior gave up six runs in the first inning, including Jose Vizcaino's three-run home run.
48.	5/24	@Houston	3-2	●		Estes claimed fourth consecutive decision. Grudzielanek went 3-for-5 and was batting .317.
49.	5/25	@Houston	7-3	●		Alou went 3-for-4 with three RBI. Zambrano picked up the win as Cubs ended road trip 8-5.
50.	5/26	Pittsburgh	10-0		●	Josh Fogg (7IP, 0 R, 3 H) outdueled Wood (7 IP, 1 R, 1H). Pirates scored nine in eighth.
51.	5/27	Pittsburgh	9-4		●	Kenny Lofton extended hitting streak to 25, while Pirates teammate Ramirez went 4-for-5.
52.	5/28	Pittsburgh	5-4	●		Pirates manager Lloyd McClendon ejected in second inning for arguing close play at first.
53.	5/30	Houston	9-1		●	Astros starter Wade Miller ruined Sosa's return with a complete-game two-hitter.
54.	5/31	Houston	1-0, (16)	●		Sosa struck out five times but broke up longest scoreless game at Wrigley with RBI in 16th.
55.	6/1	Houston	9-3		●	Wood (4-4) struck out 11 but failed to win for sixth straight start; last victory was April 29.
56.	6/3	Tampa Bay	3-2	●		Umpire Tim McClelland ejected Sosa for using a corked bat when it shattered in the first inning.
57.	6/4	Tampa Bay	5-2		●	Sosa went 1-for-4 with three strikeouts but was applauded loudly by 33,317 at Wrigley Field.
58.	6/5	Tampa Bay	8-1	●		Cubs scored seven runs in third inning. Clement improved to 3-6, allowing one run in 7 innings.
59.	6/6	NY Yankees	5-3		●	David Wells pitched Yankees to victory in club's first trip to Wrigley since 1938 World Series.
60.	6/7	NY Yankees	5-2	●		Roger Clemens vs. Wood. Clemens couldn't win 300th when Eric Karros hit two-run HR in seventh.
61.	6/8	NY Yankees	8-7	●		Cubs led 6-0 after two innings but had to hold on in ninth. Final out: Charles Gipson picked off first.
62.	6/10	@Baltimore	4-0	●		Estes (7 innings), Antonio Alfonseca and Borowski shut out Orioles. Gonzalez: 3-for-5 with a HR.
63.	6/11	@Baltimore	7-6		●	Sosa began seven-game suspension for corked-bat incident. Alou batting cleanup: 2-for-5, 2 RBI.

2003 REGULAR SEASON

GAME	DATE	OPPONENT	SCORE	WIN	LOSS	THE SKINNY
64.	6/12	@Baltimore	6-1		●	Zambrano didn't make it past second inning in game marred by two lengthy rain delays.
65.	6/13	@Toronto	5-1		●	Cubs outhit Blue Jays 12-8, but Toronto starter Kelvim Escobar struck out career-high 10.
66.	6/14	@Toronto	4-2	●		Alou hit two-run triple in first inning, while Prior improved to 8-2 and Borowski saved his 13th game.
67.	6/15	@Toronto	5-4 (10)		●	Blue Jays' Reed Johnson led off first with a homer and ended game with a 10th-inning homer.
68.	6/16	@Cincinnati	4-3	●		Alou and Karros hit back-to-back home runs in sixth inning. Borowski saved 14th in 16 chances.
69.	6/17	@Cincinnati	2-1 (10)		●	Casey beat Cubs again, this time with 10th-inning RBI single. Cubs finished 3-4 in Sosa's suspension.
70.	6/18	@Cincinnati	4-1	●		Sosa went 2-for-4 with two-run homer in return. Wood pitched complete-game three hitter.
71.	6/19	@Cincinnati	3-1		●	Farnsworth vs. Paul Wilson: Cubs reliever body-slammed Wilson in the seventh inning.
72.	6/20	White Sox	12-3		●	White Sox catcher Miguel's Olivo's grand slam highlighted six-run first inning off Estes.
73.	6/21	White Sox	7-6		●	White Sox jumped to 7-0 lead through 3 1/2 innings but had to hold on. Karros went 4-for-5.
74.	6/22	White Sox	2-1	●		Cubs rallied with two runs in eighth on Ramon Martinez's RBI double and Patterson's RBI single.
75.	6/24	Milwaukee	9-1	●		Sosa hit two of the Cubs' six homers. Others from Patterson, Wood, Grudzielanek and Gonzalez.
76.	6/25	Milwaukee	12-6 (10)		●	Former Cub Kieschnick led off 10th inning with pinch homer in Brewers' six-run inning.
77.	6/26	Milwaukee	5-3		●	Borowski blew lead for Prior (two runs in eight innings), giving up three-run HR to Geoff Jenkins.
78.	6/27	@White Sox	4-3		●	Cubs tied it in ninth, but Sox won on Jose Valentin's ninth-inning solo homer off Alfonseca.
79.	6/28	@White Sox	7-6		●	Sox scored three in final two innings and won on D'Angelo Jimenez's two-out walk-off single.
80.	6/29	@White Sox	5-2	●		Alou's two-run HR in fourth gave Cubs lead for good. Wood (8-5) allowed four hits in eight innings.
81.	6/30	@Philadelphia	4-3		●	Cubs led 3-0 through 3 1/2 innings, but Jim Thome's two-run homer in seventh won it for Phils.
82.	7/1	@Philadelphia	4-3		●	Bullpen faltered as Mike Lieberthal hit a two-out RBI single off Alfonseca in bottom of ninth.
83.	7/2	@Philadelphia	1-0	●		Sosa hit ninth-inning HR. Clement, Guthrie, Farnsworth and Borowski combined on one-hitter.
84.	7/3	@Philadelphia	12-2		●	Early July 4 fireworks for Phillies as they collected 14 hits in overcoming early 2-0 deficit.
85.	7/4	St. Louis	11-8		●	Alou hit three homers. Sosa hit his 511th, but Cardinals grabbed early 7-1 lead behind three HRs.
86.	7/5	St. Louis	6-5	●		Cubs overcame 5-0 deficit, concluding with a Gonzalez bases-loaded infield single in ninth.
87.	7/6	St. Louis	4-1		●	Woody Williams yielded six hits through 7 2/3 innings Patterson injured running out a single.
88.	7/7	Florida	6-3	●		Patterson out for season. Clement hit two-run double in three-run fourth and won game.
89.	7/8	Florida	4-3		●	With tying run on 2B with one out in ninth, Alou lined out to second and Sosa popped out.
90.	7/9	Florida	5-1	●		Wood fired three-hitter and Sosa hit a go-ahead two-run home run in the eighth inning.
91.	7/10	Atlanta	13-3		●	Estes (6-8) lost sixth consecutive decision, allowing six runs on six hits in 5 1/3 innings.
92.	7/11	Atlanta	9-5		●	Prior banged left knee into Atlanta second baseman Marcus Giles running the bases. Cubs .500.
93.	7/12	Atlanta	7-3	●		Sosa hit seventh home run in nine games, leading off six-run fourth with career No. 517.
94.	7/13	Atlanta	7-2		●	Cubs lost and headed into All-Star break 47-47, three games behind front-runner Houston.
95.	7/18	@Florida	6-0		●	Marlins starter Mark Redman struck out nine and yielded just four hits in seven innings.
96.	7/19	@Florida	1-0	●		Wood hurled second complete game in a row, allowing just two hits. Gonzalez lone RBI.
97.	7/20	@Florida	16-2	●		Marlins rookie sensation Dontrelle Willis failed to retire a Cubs batter after a 67-minute delay.
98.	7/21	@Atlanta	15-6	●		Sosa hit a three-run HR in first, finishing 3-for-4 with four RBI. Alou went 4-for-6 with five RBI.
99.	7/22	@Atlanta	8-4		●	Sergio Mitre torched for eight runs in 3 2/3 innings. Cubs traded for Ramirez and Lofton.
100.	7/23	Philadelphia	3-0		●	Phillies' Randy Wolf fired four-hit shutout, while Peoria's Thome smacked two-run HR in third.
101.	7/24	Philadelphia	14-6		●	Bobby Abreu's grand slam highlighted nine-run sixth inning for Phillies. Sosa hit 21st HR.
102.	7/25	@Houston	5-3	●		Astros led 3-0 after first inning, but Zambrano (seventh) and Alou (eighth) hit two-run homers.
103.	7/26	@Houston	3-1		●	Tim Redding allowed just two hits in seven innings, while Jeff Bagwell homered off Juan Cruz.
104.	7/27	@Houston	5-3	●		Sosa tied Willie McCovey and Ted Williams with career home run 521 with a first-inning HR.
105.	7/29	San Francisco	3-0	●		Clement (8-9) hurled two-hit shutout while striking out eight. Alou hit two-run homer in first.
106.	7/30	San Francisco	6-3		●	Giants' Edgardo Alfonzo hit a grand slam in second inning. Jason Schmidt lost no-hitter in sixth.
107.	7/31	San Francisco	9-4	●		Sosa, Alou hit two-run doubles in first. Zambrano retired Bonds with bags juiced and celebrated.
108.	8/1	Arizona	4-3 (14)	●		Both clubs scored twice in 11th. Ramirez scored Sosa with 14th-inning single for winner.
109.	8/2	Arizona	4-3		●	Borowski lost it in ninth on an Alex Cintron home run and a Raul Mondesi RBI double.
110.	8/3	Arizona	2-1	●		Sosa hit two-run homer in seventh off Oscar Villarreal for go-ahead runs. Clement now 9-9.
111.	8/5	@San Diego	3-0	●		Prior (9-5), Farnsworth, Guthrie, Remlinger and Borowski (20th save) combined on three-hitter.
112.	8/6	@San Diego	3-2	●		Sosa hit 448-foot home run, his 25th of season, while Wood struck out 10 and improved to 11-8.
113.	8/7	@San Diego	9-3	●		Sosa, Alou, Karros homered as Cubs won ninth in last 12 games. First sweep in S.D. since '93.
114.	8/8	@Los Angeles	3-1		●	Adrian Beltre's two-run homer in fifth handed Dodgers lead. Ramirez hit second HR as Cub.
115.	8/9	@Los Angeles	6-1		●	Robin Ventura's two-run homer was part of four-run L.A. first inning. Wilson Alvarez was WP.
116.	8/10	@Los Angeles	3-1	●		Sosa hit two-run homer in first and solo shot in fourth, both off Kevin Brown. Prior now 10-5.
117.	8/11	Houston	3-1		●	Wood fastest to strike out 1,000 career batters (in 134 games), but Cubs lost to Wade Miller.
118.	8/12	Houston	3-0	●		Zambrano (11-8) pitched first shutout, allowing just five hits and striking out 10. Lofton 3-for-4.
119.	8/13	Houston	6-4	●		Down 4-3, Alou ripped three-run home run in fifth inning for lead. Borowski saved 22nd.
120.	8/14	Houston	7-1	●		Gonzalez ended 2-for-46 slump with 3-for-4 performance with a homer and three RBI.
121.	8/15	Los Angeles	2-1	●		Prior threw second complete game in week, scattering seven hits as Cubs moved into first place.
122.	8/16	Los Angeles	10-5		●	Wood failed to make it out of third inn. Ramirez hit two HRs. Cubs traded for Randall Simon.
123.	8/17	Los Angeles	3-0		●	Hideo Nomo yielded just four hits through seven innings, while Eric Gagne notched 41st save.
124.	8/19	@Houston	12-8		●	Astros' Jeff Kent went 3-for-5 with a homer and six RBI. Ramirez, Alou, Gonzalez homered for Cubs.
125.	8/20	@Houston	6-0	●		Simon hit three-run homer. Ramirez added two-run shot. Prior (12-5) lost no-hitter in sixth inning.
126.	8/21	@Houston	9-3		●	Wood pulled after four innings with Astros leading 5-0 and was 1-4 with 7.31 ERA in last six starts.
127.	8/22	@Arizona	4-1	●		Zambrano lost no-hitter in eighth on questionable call at first as Shea Hillenbrand was ruled safe.
128.	8/23	@Arizona	13-2		●	Most lopsided loss of season. Estes (7-10) allowed six earned runs through 4 1/3 innings.

GAME	DATE	OPPONENT	SCORE	WIN	LOSS	THE SKINNY
129.	8/24	@Arizona	5-3	●		Borowski needed back-to-back strikeouts with bases loaded in ninth for 23rd save. Clement 11-11.
130.	8/26	@St. Louis	7-4	●		Prior claimed fifth consecutive win since coming off DL, yielding three hits in eight innings.
131.	8/27	@St. Louis	4-2		●	Wood struck out 11, but Cards scored four in eighth with go-ahead run on Farnsworth wild pitch.
132.	8/28	@St. Louis	3-2		●	Despite Sosa's 31st HR in first, Cards won on Kerry Robinson's ninth-inning HR, his first of season.
133.	8/29	Milwaukee	4-2	●		Clement fired complete game as Cubs halted Brewers' 10-game win streak.
134.	8/30	Milwaukee	9-5		●	Estes' struggles continued, allowing five runs before Baker yanked him after second inning.
135.	8/31	Milwaukee	2-0		●	Brewers right fielder Jason Conti made diving catch on Karros liner for final out with bases loaded.
136.	9/1	St. Louis	7-0	●		Six-run fifth inning. backed Prior (14-5) after 4-hour-17-minute rain delay. Karros 2-for-5 with 11th HR.
137.	9/2	St. Louis	4-2 (15)	●		Sosa's one-out, two-run homer off Jeff Fassero ended it in 15th inning of first game of DH.
138.	9/2	St. Louis	2-0		●	Morris (five hits, seven innings) outdueled Wood, who struck out nine. Cards' Jim Edmonds homered.
139.	9/3	St. Louis	8-7	●		Alou went 5-for-5 with four RBI as Cubs erased six-run deficit. Cubs a game back of Houston.
140.	9/4	St. Louis	7-6	●		Tony Womack hit go-ahead RBI single in eighth. Sosa and pitching coach Larry Rothschild ejected.
141.	9/5	@Milwaukee	4-2	●		Sosa hit two-run homer in first, his 33rd, as Cubs beat Ben Sheets again. Cruz picked up the victory.
142.	9/6	@Milwaukee	8-4	●		Simon hit three-run home run in third inning and bought entire seating section Italian sausages.
143.	9/7	@Milwaukee	9-2	●		Cubs in first by half-game after Simon's two homers for five RBI. Sosa hit No. 34. Wood won.
144.	9/9	@Montreal	4-3	●		First of three games in Puerto Rico. Cubs won sixth straight behind Alou's two-run single in seventh.
145.	9/10	@Montreal	8-4		●	Expos scored five two-out runs in eighth as Cubs fell into second, one game back of Astros.
146.	9/11	@Montreal	3-2		●	Prior's seven-game win streak snapped as rally came up short in ninth by a run. Still a game back.
147.	9/12	Cincinnati	7-6	●		Goodwin's two-run pinch-hit single in seventh inning kept Cubs on pace with Astros.
148.	9/13	Cincinnati	9-6	●		Cubs scored four in seventh for 29th comeback of year. Grudzielanek went 3-for-5. Astros won too.
149.	9/14	Cincinnati	1-0		●	Zambrano pitched great (7 IP, 4 H, 1ER), but Reds scored in ninth. Astros won, led Cubs by two.
150.	9/15	NY Mets	4-1	●		Clement (13-11) battled with strained groin in tying career high in victories. 29th save for Borowski.
151.	9/16	NY Mets	3-2	●		Prior struck out 13 in 8 2/3 innings. Borowski escaped ninth-inning jam with tying run on second.
152.	9/17	NY Mets	2-0	●		Wood (13-11) tied career high in victories. Doug Glanville and Ramirez homered. Astros led by 1/2.
153.	9/19	@Pittsburgh	10-9	●		Jason Bay finished with career-high eight RBI, but Cubs held on. Gonzalez and Ramirez homered.
154.	9/19	@Pittsburgh	10-6		●	Sosa hit 36th homer of season, but Cubs lost second game of doubleheader. Astros led by 1 1/2.
155.	9/20	@Pittsburgh	8-2		●	Pirates rookie Ryan Vogelsong held Cubs to an unearned run through seven innings. Astros lost too.
156.	9/21	@Pittsburgh	4-1	●		Prior struck out 14 through 7 2/3 innings, yielding one run on six hits. Ramirez hit 2 HRs. Astros lost.
157.	9/23	@Cincinnati	6-0	●		Cubs in first by a game as Wood lost no-hit bid in seventh on Wily Mo Pena's infield single.
158.	9/24	@Cincinnati	8-0	●		Estes shocked everyone but himself and Baker in hurling a shutout. Cubs in first by one.
159.	9/25	@Cincinnati	9-7		●	Tied with Astros after Reds' six-run sixth. Sosa passed Mickey Mantle with 537th and 538th HRs.
160.	9/27	Pittsburgh	4-2	●		Prior struck out 10 for his 18th victory in first game of doubleheader as Astros lost to Brewers.
161.	9/27	Pittsburgh	7-2	●		Cubs clinch the division. Sosa hit 40th homer in first inning, while Cubs added five runs in second.
162.	9/28	Pittsburgh	3-2		●	A day to rest starters. Bakers' first season (88-74) is a 21-game improvement from 67-95 a year ago.

Chicago Tribune

Publisher: Scott Smith
Editor: Ann Marie Lipinski
Managing editor: James O'Shea
Deputy managing editor, news: George de Lama

OUT OF THE BLUE

Editors: Dan McGrath, Kerry Luft, Bill Adee
Designers: Tony Majeri, Steven Bialer,
Steve Ravenscraft, Ted Yee
Photo editor: Todd Panagopoulos
Statistics: Keith Claxton, Lee Gordon, Johnny Rosenstein
Copy editor: Tom Carkeek
Project managers: Susan Zukrow, Bill Parker, Torry Bruno

The accounts in this book are based on the reporting of Paul Sullivan, Phil Rogers, Bonnie DeSimone, Melissa Isaacson, Bill Jauss, Dan McGrath, Fred Mitchell and John Mullin.

Photo credits

Milbert Orlando Brown: 92 (bottom)
Charles Cherney: 1, 3, 4, 6, 24 (bottom), 28, 30, 32, 33, 36, 40, 41 (top), 84, 93, 104
Nuccio DiNuzzo: Front Cover, 11, 14, 16, 47, 52, 54, 56, 73, 90, 92 (top), 94, 100 (top), 118, 119, 120, 121, Back Cover
John Lee: 114 (top)
Jose Osorio: 61, 106
Antonio Perez: 117
Scott Strazzante: 8, 10, 12, 37, 48, 65, 68 (bottom), 75, 97, 100 (bottom) 115, 116
Nancy Stone: 23
Bonnie Trafelet: 41 (bottom), 82, 108, 109, 114 (bottom), 120
Phil Velasquez: 19, 21, 25, 26, 27, 34, 38, 42, 44, 45, 50, 53, 55, 58, 60, 62, 68 (top), 71, 72, 74, 76, 78, 79, 80, 83, 86 (bottom), 87, 88, 89, 98, 101, 102, 110, 111, 112